Unstoppable

UNSTOPPABLE

A Life of Purpose, Passion, and Perseverance

Bratati Ganguly, PhD, MBA, BCMASc

©2025 All Rights Reserved. No portion of this book may be reproduced, stored in a retrieval system, or transmitted in any form or by any means—electronic, mechanical, photocopy, recording, scanning, or other—except for brief quotations in critical reviews or articles without the prior permission of the author.

Published by Game Changer Publishing

Disclaimer: This book is a reflection of my lived experience—the moments that shaped me, challenged me, and guided my growth. While I have endeavored to share these stories with honesty and care, memory is inherently personal, often colored by emotion and perspective. The events are presented as I remember and feel them, which may differ from how others might recall them. Still, the essence of each narrative remains true: a tribute to resilience, agency, and the enduring power of one's voice.

To honor the privacy of individuals involved, names and identifying details have been altered where appropriate. This book does not aim to chronicle history in a conventional sense, but rather to illuminate the truth of my journey. Not every event in my life has been recounted here; instead, I have chosen to highlight a few moments—that I believe carry meaning, inspiration, and the message I hope to leave with my readers.

Paperback ISBN: 978-1-968250-62-1
Hardcover ISBN: 978-1-968250-63-8
Digital ISBN: 978-1-968250-64-5

www.GameChangerPublishing.com

Dedication

To my parents, Debabrata and Sadhana—

Your unwavering love, enduring sacrifices, and the values you instilled in me are the foundation of all I am and all I strive to be. Your strength is my compass—guiding me through yesterday, anchoring me today, and lighting the way for tomorrow.

To my husband, Shrikant—

My steadfast partner and source of unshakable support. Your belief in me—even in moments when I faltered—has lifted me higher than I ever imagined. Together, we've turned dreams into milestones.

To my daughter, Aadrika—

You gave me the gift of motherhood and filled my world with light. I hope I can inspire you and be your role model. May you always chase your dreams with boldness, grace, and the fierce joy that lives within your heart.

To all my mentors and friends—

I would not be the professional I am today without your unwavering support and belief in me. I am deeply grateful our paths crossed, and I will always cherish the moments we shared—learning, growing, and evolving together.

With all my love, always.

Bratati

Read This First

Thank you for taking the time to read my book — it truly means a lot. I'd be delighted to connect with you and continue the conversation beyond the pages.

Scan the QR Code Here:

Unstoppable

A Life of Purpose, Passion, and Perseverance

Bratati Ganguly
PhD, MBA, BCMASc

Breaking Barriers, Balancing Life, and Redefining Success

Foreword

It is an extraordinary privilege to pen the foreword to a book that is not merely a life story but a testament to the unyielding spirit of a woman who dared to rise above all odds, blaze her own trail, and leave behind a path illuminated for countless others to follow. This is the life story of my wife, Bratati—a woman whose journey is defined not by privilege or shortcuts, but by struggle, hard work, passion, and unwavering perseverance.

From the earliest days of her life, Bratati was no stranger to adversity. Born into a world where the odds were seldom in favor of a girl child, she learned early on that she would have to fight—not just for opportunity, but for recognition, respect, and even her voice. Yet she never backed down. Where doors were closed, she found windows. Where paths didn't exist, she created them.

This book chronicles the trials and triumphs of a woman who refused to accept limitations. In the face of societal expectations that sought to confine her to predefined roles, she dreamt bigger. In the face of professional environments that tested her resolve, she stood firmer. And in moments of personal and professional doubt—moments that could have easily broken her spirit—she chose resilience over retreat.

What makes her story deeply compelling is not that she reached a position of influence and impact, but how she got there: with authenticity, compassion, and a relentless work ethic. She balanced ambition with empathy, assertiveness with grace, and determination with humility. Her life is not a tale of overnight success. It is a tapestry woven with years of sacrifice, sleepless nights, hard-earned achievements, and quiet victories that the world may never see, but which shaped her into the remarkable woman she is today.

Every chapter of her journey speaks to young girls who are told they "can't," to women professionals who feel unseen in boardrooms, to mothers trying to juggle family and careers, and to dreamers held back by doubt. Her story says one thing, loud and clear: you are enough. With courage, dedication, and a fire in your heart, no mountain is too high, no goal too far.

This book is also a celebration of values that are too often overlooked in the pursuit of success—integrity, kindness, and the strength to uplift others even as you climb your own ladder. Through her journey, Bratati has not only carved a legacy of personal achievement but has also become a beacon for those around her by mentoring, supporting, and inspiring countless women to believe in themselves.

As her partner in life, I have witnessed her struggles and her rise firsthand. I have seen the quiet battles, the tears behind closed doors, the decisions made in solitude, and the unspoken courage it took to face each new day with purpose. But I have also seen her laugh without fear, love without condition, and lead with a heart full of conviction. That is the woman behind these pages.

Her life may be singular, but the values and vision it carries belong to every girl who dreams, every woman who strives, and every soul that seeks to live a life of meaning. I hope this book finds you at the right time and reminds you that in a world full of noise, your story matters too.

With pride, love, and deepest admiration

– Shrikant Shenoy, VP Financial Services

Table of Contents

	Introduction	1
Chapter 1	My Childhood: The Burden of Legacy	7
Chapter 2	The Revolt for Higher Education	17
Chapter 3	Independent Life in Pune: A New World	29
Chapter 4	From India to America: A Journey of Resilience, Purpose, and Triumph	45
Chapter 5	New Beginnings in New Jersey: A Bold Leap Balancing Love, Career, and the Pursuit of Purpose	55
Chapter 6	The Transformative Journey of Motherhood: Balancing Ambition, Love, and Self-Discovery	69
Chapter 7	My MBA Journey: Balancing Motherhood, Ambition, and Growth	85
Chapter 8	Beyond the Pandemic: Resolving to Build Meaningful Connections	97
Chapter 9	Laying My Medical Affairs Foundations: A Journey of Purpose, Passion, and Perseverance	107
Chapter 10	Breaking Barriers: A Woman's Journey to Serial Entrepreneurship and Growth in Medical Affairs	125
Chapter 11	Retrospection: Echoes of the Past	137
	Conclusion	157

Introduction

It was one of those rare, quiet nights. The kind where time feels slower, and the noise of the world softens into the background. My daughter and I sat curled up on the couch, the warm glow of a table lamp casting soft shadows on the walls as we talked, just the two of us. I found myself reminiscing, almost unintentionally, sharing stories from my life that I'd rarely spoken aloud. Stories of the hurdles I had to leap over, the times I was underestimated, and the moments I had to find my voice in rooms where it wasn't invited. I shared about choices I made as a woman, a mother, and a professional, carving my place in spaces that weren't built for me.

She listened with wide eyes and the kind of attentiveness that only children have when they sense something important is being said. And then, with a quiet certainty that pierced through the stillness, she asked, "Mom, you have so many stories to share. Why don't you write a book and share it with the world?"

For a moment, I couldn't speak. Her words hung in the air like a whisper from the universe, something I didn't know I was waiting to hear until I heard it. It was as if everything I had lived through—every challenge, every detour, every step forward and two steps backward—was all pointing me toward this very moment. A moment of clarity and purpose. In that instant, I knew I had to write this book, not just for me but for all the women out there who need to hear that they can break free from societal limitations, just as I did.

That night, long after she had gone to bed, I sat in silence and stared at a blank page. In my mind's eye, I could see the page filled with joy and pain, vulnerability and victory, and the kind of raw truth we so often bury beneath expectations. I realized that these weren't just my stories. They were our stories—echoes of every woman who has ever been told she was "too much" or "not enough." Every woman who has carried silent dreams in her heart while juggling responsibilities in her hands. Every woman who has dared to choose herself, even when the world demanded otherwise.

This book was born that night. Not out of ambition, but out of necessity. A necessity to speak, to share, to inspire.

My name is Dr. Bratati Ganguly, and my journey began in a small town in Kolkata, India, where I nurtured big dreams that fueled my aspirations. I dared to dream big when there was no precedent, no one to guide me, and the odds seemed stacked against me. I am a success story, proof that it is possible to create your own path, even when there is no support system or roadmap to follow. With unwavering purpose, relentless passion, and sheer perseverance, I forged an innovative career path for myself. I wrote this book to tell you that if I can do it, so can you.

This book is not a collection of my accolades or a celebration of my achievements, but rather a tool for inspiration. My hope is that some part of my journey will resonate with you and that you can draw inspiration in your own life from the strategies, tactics, and lessons I've learned along the way.

The journey I share is one of defying limitations, pushing past self-doubt, and daring to dream bigger than anyone thought possible. My professional and personal goals have always been grounded in the belief that success is not just about achieving but about honoring and valuing the lives we nurture and the stories we create along the way. It's a testament to what you can achieve when you take control of your own story and refuse to be defined by circumstances or societal expectations.

I have spent my adult life traveling and living across continents, and today I'm a serial entrepreneur with a deep passion for making a meaningful impact. I wear many hats, from CEO to strategic partner, medical affairs leader, podcast host, wife, and mother. Above all these, I cherish my daughter every single day, and I celebrate her life with immense love and gratitude, recognizing the unique beauty in her spirit. This book is for her.

This book is for all young girls. This book is for ambitious women, mothers, and those who support them—the parents and partners who recognize the audacity, fierce determination, and dreams of fearless women. It is for those who dare to dream beyond the confines of social and cultural norms, for those who are ready to break barriers and make their mark on the world.

Whether you are a young girl discovering your potential, a woman on the path to greatness, or a mother balancing it all, your efforts are a tribute to your strength and ambition. Success is not reserved for a select few but is achievable by anyone willing to put in the hard work, challenge their limitations, and stay true to their vision. Let this book be the catalyst that helps you structure your path, implement your strategies, and, ultimately, achieve the success you deserve.

As I share my story, my deepest desire is to inspire women never to give up, even when the path feels lonely and their support systems seem non-existent. The strength to persevere lives within you, and self-reliance is the key to moving forward. You hold in your hands not just chapters of my life, but fragments of yours too. Stories that remind us that breaking barriers isn't about being fearless—it's about rising above, despite the fear. It's about rewriting the narrative that says we must fit into boxes we never built.

This book is my gift to the women who are still waiting for permission to rise, and for those who have already begun but need a hand to hold as they climb higher. It serves as a reminder that, no matter the obstacles, the strength to rise above them is within you. Take that next step, break those barriers, and create your own path to success.

I hope you will walk away from this book not only inspired but also ignited with the fire to take action. My vision for you is that by the end of these pages, you will feel empowered, confident, and ready to embrace your potential.

The power to create the life you've always dreamed of is already within you. This is your call to action. Don't wait for permission. Don't wait for the perfect moment. Step into your greatness. Take bold strides forward and build the life you deserve. It's your time to shine, and this book is here to remind you that nothing is impossible when you refuse to give up on yourself.

So here it is—my story, your story, our story. A story of becoming. A story of rising.

Welcome to the beginning.

CHAPTER 1

My Childhood: The Burden of Legacy

My journey begins with my parents, two extraordinary people whose achievements and legacy shaped my life. My father, the epitome of achievement, was a highly educated man who studied Computer Science at the prestigious Indian Institute of Technology (IIT), often referred to as the MIT of India. He was well-rounded, excelling in academics, sports, and leadership, and he held a top-ranked executive position in the government sector within our community. His journey was one of relentless effort.

His legacy was significant—he was the first in our family to reach such heights, a pioneer whose success became a beacon for those who followed. In our community, he was a respected leader and the president of a community cultural organization that people turned to for advice in times of need. His achievements afforded us a life of luxury, from a sprawling bungalow with four bedrooms and an expansive patio to a household of dedicated staff managing daily tasks. Amidst this privilege, our values remained grounded in our traditions and the belief in personal responsibility. We were taught that while faith in God was important, achieving one's dreams required perseverance and self-reliance.

My mother, in contrast to my father, was a simple, petite woman—someone who, by societal standards, seemed to fit the mold of a traditional homemaker. However, as you will learn, she is a woman of immense determination and resilience. She exuded quiet strength, gracefully navigating life's complexities while ensuring that her daughters grew up with confidence and aspirations.

Our family followed deep-rooted traditions, celebrating Durga Puja, Diwali, and Christmas with grandeur. Our cultural fabric was rich with colors, flavors, and festivities. Durga Puja is a festival honoring the goddess Durga, who symbolizes the triumph of good over evil. For Bengalis, it's the cultural equivalent of Christmas, Thanksgiving, and the Fourth of July rolled into one. It brings families together, marks the victory of hope, and reminds us of the strength of the feminine divine. The scent of sandalwood incense, the rustle of new silk sarees, and the rhythmic beat of the dhaak—a traditional Bengali drum—were the signs that Durga Puja had arrived. Growing up in a Bengali household in India, the festival was more than just a celebration; it was the heartbeat of our community, a five-day embodiment of faith, art, and togetherness.

Despite the grandeur of the festival, our parents—my mother, with her quiet elegance, and my father, with his disciplined calm—used these days not just to celebrate, but to ground us. I remember one year, I must have been around ten years old, my elder sister and I were engrossed in getting ready with the new clothes for Saptami, the second day of the festival. We twirled in front of the mirror, admiring ourselves, when my dad walked in. He smiled, then asked gently, "Did you remember to give the new clothes to our staff?"

We hadn't. Caught up in the thrill of the new clothes, shoes, and hair clips, we had forgotten the very lesson they had quietly taught every year: celebration must be accompanied by compassion. He didn't scold us. Instead, he helped us pack the new clothes, making sure each of our helpers received their yearly bonus and new clothes on the auspicious occasion of Durga Puja. "Joy means nothing," he said, "unless shared."

That same year, my mom woke us at 5:00 a.m. for anjali—the prayer offering. The community temple was packed, the air thick with the fragrance of flowers and incense. I yawned in protest, groggy and irritable. My mom just smiled, pressed a warm luchi (fried bread) into my hand as a bribe, and whispered, "Goddess Durga fought for us without sleep. You can manage one morning." I didn't know then that this was her way of teaching endurance.

We were fortunate. We attended a convent school, always had delicious food on the table, and the rooms of our house were filled with books to read. But my parents never let privilege make us forget gratitude. My dad would often say, "You are not better than anyone else. You are simply better placed to help." And my mom, ever gentle, reminded us that a life lived sincerely, even quietly, can move mountains.

Looking back, it wasn't just the shimmering lights of Diwali or the joyous hymns of Christmas carols that shaped me—it was these small, quiet moments during Durga Puja that built my compass. A compass that always pointed toward humility, sincerity, and hard work. My parents consistently instilled these values in us. They believed in staying rooted despite success and always being honest in their endeavors.

My mother named me Bratati, a name imbued with purpose. It means "one who is devoted to a mission." Indeed, my life has been a series of missions—some chosen, some bestowed upon me by fate. The first and most personal has been to uphold my family name, to ensure that its legacy endures through me. This mission, this commitment, is an inseparable part of my identity, one that I will honor for as long as I live. A name is more than a mere string of letters; it is a story, a history, a belonging. I have chosen to carry mine, just as a son would, with pride, purpose, and an unyielding sense of devotion.

My childhood was filled with opportunities. I attended one of the best convent schools, where I was encouraged to excel academically and explore my interests. Our community was progressive, fostering an environment where children could flourish in arts, education, and sports.

A typical day in my childhood was filled with joy and ambition. I would wake up excited to go to school, eager to learn and share my knowledge with teachers and friends. My academic achievements brought pride to my family, and my mother was my biggest cheerleader. After school, I would return home, where I would study and practice my extracurricular activities with enthusiasm. Life seemed picture-perfect until the birth of my younger sister, the third daughter in the family.

To an outsider, my life seemed perfect, with access to the best education, cultural exposure, and a supportive family. Behind closed doors, we faced a harsh reality: gender bias. My mother gave birth to three daughters, and despite our family's achievements, society looked down upon us. My mother bore the brunt of criticism for not giving birth to a son. This stark contrast between external admiration and internal struggle was my first encounter with the deep-rooted gender issues in our society. My younger sister's birth in particular changed everything. In my community growing up, having two daughters in a family was met with begrudging acceptance. Three daughters, however—that was unacceptable. For the first time in my life, our family was ridiculed. People laughed at us, mocked my mother, and questioned the worth of my sisters and me simply because we were daughters.

This moment shattered my idealized world and exposed me to the silent yet crushing expectations that society imposed on women.

I have a vivid memory of being twelve years old, standing on the community auditorium stage and clutching a gleaming trophy almost as tall as I was. I had just been named the "Sports Champion of the Year" after winning first place in all four events I competed in that day. As my name was called out over the microphone, applause thundered through the hall, echoing like a drumbeat in my chest. From the crowd, I spotted my mother, her eyes glistening with tears. She wiped them away with the edge of her sari. At that moment, I felt invincible. I had done something that mattered—something that would make our entire family proud.

Later that evening, back at home, my mom carefully placed the trophy on the shelf, lining it up beside the other awards I had earned over the years. My dad offered a quiet smile, his pride subtle but unmistakable. We settled down for evening tea, warmth and satisfaction filling the air. A relative came over for a visit, one of many who never hid their disapproval of our "daughters-only" family.

"Very nice," she said, nodding at the trophy. "But still, all this means little without a son to carry on the family name."

I saw my mother's face falter, just for a moment, before she quickly composed herself. But I had seen enough. Behind her poised silence, I recognized the sting of yet another wound inflicted by tradition, the kind of pain that doesn't raise its voice but lingers in the heart.

My victory, which only hours earlier had felt like a soaring triumph, now seemed to dissolve in the shadow of an expectation I could never fulfill. For the first time, I understood the fragile line between celebration and shame when society insists you are born into the "wrong" gender.

That night, sleep evaded me. I lay awake, replaying those words over and over, feeling the weight of something ancient and unjust settle onto my small shoulders.

By morning, I had made a decision. I rose earlier than usual, laid out my books, scribbled a fresh list of goals, and made a silent promise to myself: If they cannot see the worth of a daughter, I will become undeniable.

From then on, I studied harder. I trained longer. Each time someone questioned my worth, each whisper or sideways glance, I used it as fuel. Not out of anger, but out of deep, enduring love for my mother, who deserved more than veiled scorn and polite disappointment.

Over the years, the shelf grew crowded with medals, certificates, and trophies, but I never forgot that day—the day I realized that even the brightest spotlight can't chase away every shadow. Sometimes, it's what you choose to do after the applause fades that defines who you truly become.

My mother, a woman of immense strength, understood the unspoken judgments we faced as women and saw the struggles ahead for us. She knew that despite our innocence, we were being made to bear the weight of societal prejudices—treated as if our mere existence was a flaw, a punishment for something we had no control over. Some even dared to say that my mother was a sinner because she had not given birth to a son. Can you imagine? A child, too young to comprehend the depth of such cruelty, being told that her mother was at fault simply because she had daughters and not a son?

I remember the day I ran home, tears streaming down my cheeks, gasping for breath between sobs. I had overheard a group of neighbors whispering just loud enough for me to hear—mocking my mother for having three daughters, pitying her misfortune as if we were burdens to be endured rather than children to be cherished.

Their words pierced deeper than I expected. I was only a child, but I already knew the sting of being "less than" in a world that worshipped sons. I burst through the front door and collapsed into my mother's arms, repeating their words through my sobs, unsure if I was angry, ashamed, or both.

She didn't flinch. Her embrace was steady, and her voice, when it came, was firm and unwavering.

"Let them say what they want," she said, wiping my tears gently with the edge of her sari. "You are not here to please the world. You are here to rise. To shine. To build the life they said you could never have."

I looked up at her, still sniffling, and saw in her eyes not defeat but fire.

"Push yourself," she continued, her voice growing stronger with every word. "Never look back. Never hold back. The sky is your limit, and if they cannot see your light, shine brighter until they have no choice."

At that moment, something shifted in me. I was no longer just a girl trying to belong. I was a force in the making. I was armed with my mother's faith, her strength stitched into every corner of my heart.

Looking back, I realize that my mother wasn't simply fighting for us; she was fighting through us. With every achievement, every milestone, I wasn't just proving my worth—I was echoing hers.

From that moment on, I stopped holding back. I carried her words with me like armor. Not just in moments of doubt, but in every exam hall, every competition, every quiet hour spent studying when the rest of the world was asleep. Her voice became the constant rhythm behind my ambition. If I had pushed myself twice as hard before, now I was pushing ten times harder. I excelled in academics, determined to prove that my intellect and ambition were as valuable as those of any boy. After my younger sister was born, my resolve only strengthened. I had to prove that we, as daughters, were just as precious, just as capable, just as worthy.

I found solace in the arts, channeling my passion into classical dance. Inspired by my childhood best friend, Mira, I asked to learn Kathak (a classical Indian dance form) and quickly rose to distinction, earning diplomas and accolades. My achievements in dance were just one facet of my journey. I immersed myself in music, earning distinction in

Rabindra Sangeet, a revered classical form of Indian music. My hands brought life to canvases through painting, garnering praise from my art teacher. I even went on to earn a diploma in Painting & Arts. I embraced theater, carrying forward a family legacy, earning recognition for my performances in community plays during Durga Puja. I thrived in athletics, competing in relay races and sprinting events, proving my physical prowess. On Sports Day, an annual event held in my community, I became the undisputed champion, winning every event and setting a record that earned me the Championship award, which remains unbroken to this day.

I was well-rounded, just like my father, not only for personal satisfaction but to challenge the very foundation of the societal norms that sought to diminish my worth. I even kept my hair short like a boy at my parents' indirect suggestion, so that I would look tough and determined. My name became known, and my achievements were acknowledged within my community and among my father's circle of colleagues, friends, and family. And yet, deep down, I knew this was never just about me. It was about proving a point: As a girl, I am no less than any boy. My value is undeniable.

My warrior mindset was born from necessity. I was always ready—ready to fight, ready to prove, ready to rise above expectations. At every step, my mother stood by me, and her words were a constant reminder that I was meant for greatness. Together, we turned adversity into opportunity, transforming pain into fuel for success.

We could have succumbed to the weight of societal judgment. We could have drowned in despair, let their words break us, and allowed their prejudices to define us. But we chose a different path. We chose to fight, to rise, to shine. We refused to let outdated beliefs dictate our worth. Instead, we redefined it on our own terms.

Looking back, I am grateful—not for the unfair treatment but for the resilience it built within me. This journey was never about seeking validation; it was about rewriting the narrative. And I did, with my mother by my side.

My story is one of privileges intertwined with struggle. While I had access to the best education and upbringing, I also witnessed the challenges that came with being a girl in a society that undervalued daughters. It was in these moments of contrast that I found my strength, determination, and the desire to challenge the norms that sought to define my worth.

> **My message for young girls:** Self-motivation is the driving force behind your dreams, but the unwavering support of your parents serves as the foundation upon which you build your success. The path may be challenging and filled with obstacles and uncertainties, but with perseverance and the right mindset, you will rise above every hurdle.
>
> Never waver, and never lose faith, for true success belongs to those who never give up. Please remember this and never give up on yourself or any other girl or woman. What we all need is a helping hand to nudge us along on our journey.

CHAPTER 2

The Revolt for Higher Education

As I grew up, I became a force to be reckoned with—fierce, determined, and ready to take on the world. Excelling in academics, sports, theater, painting, dance, and singing, I became the poster child for success in my family, embodying the "like father, like daughter" sentiment. I built on my father's shields of achievement with many of my own. He set the benchmark, and I was determined to surpass it, continuously striving to become the best version of myself.

Despite the comfort and privileges at home, I knew deep down that staying within those walls would limit my potential. The path was paved for me. My education, environment, and future in India were secure, but I had a vision that extended beyond the familiar. I longed to break free, to step out of my comfort zone, and to explore the limitless possibilities that awaited me. I didn't know how, when, or where, but I had to go beyond the life that my parents and society had neatly laid out for me.

When I first shared my dream of pursuing higher education away from home, my mother was both thrilled and terrified. She understood me because she, too, had once dreamed of defying the expectations placed on her. As a young girl, my mother had a quiet fire within her. She loved political science and medicine and longed to become a doctor, to make something out of her own life. She had imagined a life of purpose beyond the walls of her home, filled with books, stimulating conversations with peers, and independence. But her dreams never got the chance to take flight.

Married at a young age, before she could complete her education, she was pulled into the rhythm of family duties and societal expectations. In a world where a woman's ambitions were often seen as luxuries rather than necessities, her desires were slowly silenced. Not with cruelty, but with the gentle, relentless pressure of tradition, where she quietly tucked away her dreams for the sake of duty.

Still, that fire never truly went out.

She now saw a reflection of her younger self in me—restless, curious, determined. My dreams had become hers, carried forward on the wings she was never given. And together, without ever needing to speak it aloud, we made a silent pact: Nothing would stop us. Her unrealized hopes fueled my resolve, and my victories became her redemption.

We refused to let society dictate what my future should look like. My education, my ambitions, and my right to dream were not up for negotiation. Through me, she lived a life she once only imagined. And through her, I carried a legacy of resilience, sacrifice, and a deep, unyielding belief that a girl's dreams are worth fighting for.

Breaking the news to my father felt like standing at the edge of a storm.

I still remember that evening clearly—how the warm smell of incense from the prayer room mingled with the tension in the air. My mother and I sat across from him at the dinner table, and with a mix of courage and fear, I said the words that would change everything: "Dad, I want to leave home to study."

He looked up slowly, as if he hadn't heard me right. Then, his face darkened.

"What are you saying?" he asked, his voice low but rising steadily. "No one—no one—in this family has ever done such a thing. Not the boys, not the girls. And you want to go?"

I could feel his disappointment crashing into anger. He was furious. What I was asking was unheard of. He pushed back from the table, pacing the floor. "What will people say?" he shouted. "A girl? Living alone? This is how families lose their honor. This is how daughters lose their way." How could a young girl, a minor, be trusted to take care of herself in an unknown city? He sought advice from others, but all he received were warnings: "She will ruin the family name." "This is a disaster waiting to happen." "A girl cannot be given such freedom."

His words cut deep, not just because of what he said, but because I knew he was speaking from fear. Fear of judgment, fear of failure, fear of letting go. He wasn't just battling me; he was battling generations of beliefs.

I stood frozen, unsure how to respond. But my mother did not flinch.

"Let them say what they want," she said softly but firmly. "If we raise our daughters only to keep them confined, then what exactly are we protecting?"

He turned to her, stunned into silence for a moment. She had always been quiet, never one to contradict him in front of others. But this time, something in her had shifted.

"She has earned this," my mom continued. "She has worked hard. She wants to study, to grow, to build something for herself. You may fear for her, but I believe in her." He didn't answer right away. He sat down heavily in his chair, staring at the floor, wrestling with emotions too heavy for words. That night was a night that changed everything for me.

My mother stood by me like a pillar, unwavering. She made an extraordinary declaration: "I guarantee her success. She will bring nothing but pride to our family." Her faith in me was unshakable. She was my shield as I prepared for battle.

That night, I staged the first act of rebellion in my life.

I pushed my plate away and quietly left the dinner table. My dad didn't say a word, but I could feel his gaze following me as I walked to my room. I closed the door softly behind me, then pulled out a chair and sat upright with my back straight and my fists clenched in my lap. I wasn't angry. I was resolute.

I refused to cry. I refused to sleep. I refused to bend.

For hours, the house went quiet. The fan hummed above me, the night outside wrapped itself around the windows, but I didn't move. At one point, my mother knocked gently. When she opened the door and saw me still sitting there in the dim light, she didn't try to stop me. She placed a shawl around my shoulders and whispered, "He'll see. Just hold on."

I stayed that way the entire night, my body aching but my resolve stronger than ever. This wasn't just about going away for higher studies anymore. This was about being heard. This was about standing up for every silent "no" I had been told.

The next morning, as the sun spilled into my room, I was still there, sleepless and hungry, but unmoved. My father stood in the doorway. His eyes softened as he took in the sight of me, still in the same chair, still waiting.

We didn't speak right away. He stepped inside, sat down on the edge of my bed, and looked at me. Not with anger this time, but with something else. Worry. Uncertainty.

Then my mother came in, gently but firmly breaking the silence. "If you need someone to blame, blame me," she said. "But let her go. She's not asking to leave you behind. She's asking to become who she's meant to be."

He didn't respond right away, but something shifted at that moment. The walls of tradition didn't come crashing down, but they cracked, just enough to let in the first light. He still had his doubts, but he saw the fire within me. He knew this was not a whim but a calling.

When he gave his consent, the floodgates of emotion opened within me. I cried uncontrollably, overwhelmed by a mix of hope, relief, and a profound sense of possibility. But before the tears came, I remember the exact moment—the way he stood, hands clasped behind his back, avoiding my eyes.

He didn't say "I'm proud of you." He didn't say "I believe in you." That wasn't his way.

Instead, in a quiet, almost gruff voice, he said, "If you must go, then go. But remember who you are. Don't forget your roots. And whatever you do, don't bring shame to your family." That was it.

But I heard everything I needed in those few words. Buried beneath caution was an acknowledgment of my strength. Behind the warning was a guarded blessing wrapped in fear, pride, and protection—a father's unspoken love.

My mother stood beside him, tears already in her eyes. She reached for my hand and held it as long as she could. That single moment held the weight of generations—the bending of tradition, the silent power of maternal support, and the cautious hope of a man learning to let go.

I sat there, tears rolling freely down my face, not because I was sad, but because I finally saw the path ahead. A door had opened, and I was ready to walk through it.

I knew that stepping into the unknown was daunting, but I never feared failure. My vision was clear. I wanted to do something unprecedented, something that no one in our family had ever done before. My conviction overpowered any doubts. I believed in myself, my values, and my ability to navigate uncharted territory without compromising my integrity. I never forgot my mother's words, "I guarantee her success. She will bring nothing but pride to our family." They became my guiding principle.

I decided to attend the University of Pune, India (approximately two thousand miles from my home in Bengal) because Pune is known as the "Oxford of the East." In pursuit of better educational and overall growth, Pune was the place for me. Realizing I was about to leave behind everything I knew was a monumental shift, one that felt both exhilarating and terrifying. It was hard to believe—a small-town girl setting off on a journey that no one in my family had ever dared to take. I knew this was the first step toward fulfilling my dreams.

My community was skeptical. Whispers followed me like shadows. They were curious, but also disapproving and sharp-edged. The day I left home with a suitcase in hand and dreams in my heart, I could feel eyes watching from behind half-closed doors and curtained windows. A neighbor aunty, who had always greeted me with sweet words, muttered to my mother, "Sending a girl so far away is asking for trouble. She'll either come back ashamed or never come back at all."

These weren't just idle remarks. They were warnings, predictions, judgments dressed as concern. Even the local shopkeeper, who had watched me grow up, shook his head and told my father, "You're being too lenient. Girls from good families don't live alone."

Society stood at the edge of our ambition, expectant and cynical, poised to declare, "We told you so." They waited—not with concern, but with a quiet eagerness—for our misstep, our unraveling, our failure to align with the limits they had quietly prescribed. But my mother and I remained unmoved. We did not flinch beneath the weight of their doubt; instead, we gathered it like kindling, letting their skepticism ignite the fire that propelled us forward.

A desire to fit in or to seek their approval did not inform our actions. Conformity held no appeal. What we sought was far more radical: to disrupt, to transcend, to reimagine the possibilities for those who had long been told to dream smaller. Ours was not a rebellion for rebellion's sake; it was a purposeful defiance, rooted in love, courage, and an unshakable belief in what could be.

We were not simply trying to prove them wrong. That would have been too small a victory. Our mission was larger, bolder: to write a new narrative—one that belonged not only to us, but to every girl who had ever been told "no", and still dared to imagine "yes".

I'm a mother now, and I understand my father's fears. I recognize that his concerns were shaped not only by societal pressures but also by his deep-seated love and desire for protection. But I also know that courage and determination can break even the strongest chains of convention. Challenging traditional norms was not just a bold step; it was a monumental shift for my family.

Looking back, I see the ripple effect of that decision. My cousins, sisters, extended family, and even the broader community have witnessed my journey. Due to my success story, many young women have now dared to step out on their own, away from home, to pursue higher education. Our success stories have traveled across miles, reaching homes where parents once hesitated to send their daughters away for advanced studies. Today, those very parents have become champions of their daughters' ambitions, encouraging them to dream beyond societal confines.

So, against all odds, I stepped forward—not merely for myself, but as a voice, a symbol, for every girl who had ever been told she couldn't, who had been asked to shrink herself to fit into someone else's vision of what was possible. With each step, I carried their silenced dreams and my own quiet defiance, refusing to be defined by the narrow expectations society had crafted for people like me.

Had my journey unraveled the way they had predicted—had I faltered, as they so confidently assumed I would—the road behind me would have collapsed, not just for me, but for every young woman daring to follow. That is the burden and the blessing of being first: Your success becomes the blueprint, your failure the cautionary tale. But I refused to let their story be the final word.

It wasn't luck that brought me here. It was relentless perseverance stitched with sincerity, the courage to be strategic when passion wasn't enough, and the kind of hard work that happens quietly when no one is watching. People like me don't inherit open doors; we push them open, we walk through, and we leave them ajar for those who come after.

In doing so, we haven't just defied expectations; we've reimagined them. We've rewritten the narrative entirely.

※

When I first returned home after proving I could make it on my own, there was a moment of disbelief. Those who had once doubted me, who had expected my dreams to crumble under the weight of the unknown, could not fathom my success. I had stepped into a world without resources, without a blueprint, yet I had survived—and thrived. The recognition I received became a point of pride for my parents. They boasted about my achievements to everyone they knew, and our community of family and friends, caught between admiration and envy, could no longer ignore my story.

Being a pioneer in breaking societal expectations is an honor, but it comes with immense responsibility. It is not enough to take the first step; you must ensure you never falter. As you soar, your feet must remain firmly on the ground. Every single day, you must remind yourself that you are, knowingly or unknowingly, someone's role model. Eyes are on you—watching, learning, drawing courage from your journey. You cannot afford to lose sight of your goals. You carry the hopes of those who once hesitated, of those who now dare because you did first.

However, no woman who breaks barriers does so alone. If you believe that you can do everything on your own, you are living in an illusion. A strong support system is essential. For me, that foundation was my mother. Seeking support does not diminish one's strength; it fortifies it. It empowers you to keep pushing forward.

My first dream—stepping away from the comfort of home to pursue my education independently—was a defining moment. It revealed my true potential, proving to the world and myself what I was capable of achieving. But that was only the beginning. The need to overcompensate and prove my worth never truly ended. It continues to fuel me, driving me forward.

Achieving higher education in Pune was not just an academic milestone; it was a testament to my resilience. It reinforced my belief that I have much more to accomplish, that my potential is boundless. To be among the first to envision something, to execute it despite immense pressure and doubt, and to rise above it all—that experience is transformative. It strengthens your belief in yourself and teaches you that the greatest victories are born in the face of the greatest resistance.

My message for young girls who are pondering whether to spread their wings and fly: Every girl should dare to dream big, regardless of where she comes from. Your environment, city, gender, or family background should neither limit your aspirations nor define your worth. The sky should be your only limit. To turn dreams into reality, you must inspire and convince your family to support your journey. With determination, resilience, and unwavering belief in yourself, you can achieve anything you set your heart on. Dream boldly, pursue that dream relentlessly, and make it happen.

CHAPTER 3

Independent Life in Pune: A New World

As I prepared to leave my family and my comfort zone, I had the sudden realization that I would be two thousand miles away from the safety net of my parents' support. The tearful, joyous relief that I was going to live out my dreams gave way to the intimidating reality of what lay ahead. I could no longer simply walk into my mother's comforting embrace or seek my father's advice. The independence I was stepping into, though a dream realized, came with its own set of challenges. I had to live on my own, manage my meals, my studies, and every little detail of life that had once seemed trivial. It was a massive shift—emotionally, physically, and psychologically.

The magnitude of this transformation didn't hit me all at once. At first, I convinced myself it would be fine. I could compartmentalize my emotions, something I had always been good at, and I kept telling myself that everything would work out.

However, once I arrived in Pune, the cultural shock was immediate, marked by a stark contrast between everything I had known and the new environment I was entering. The people's ways of thinking, celebrating, and interacting were unfamiliar to me. The food, so much spicier than the sweet dishes I was accustomed to, made my body rebel. Being surrounded by people who spoke a different dialect, with no common language to fall back on, was another wall I had to scale.

One of the earliest and most difficult moments came during my first week of classes. I had signed up for a chemistry lab slot and arrived on time, nervously clutching my notes. I was hoping to partner with someone—anyone—so I wouldn't have to go through the exercise alone. But when I asked a group of girls (my classmates) standing together if I could join them, they looked at one another, exchanged a few words in Marathi, and shook their heads politely. "Already full," one said curtly, though I knew that wasn't entirely true. I smiled awkwardly and stepped back, pretending I didn't care.

But I did. That moment stung, not because I was rejected, but because it made me feel invisible. I ended up working alone that day, fumbling with the glassware and second-guessing every measurement while trying to fight back tears. I felt foreign, out of place. The proud girl who had once walked onstage to the sound of applause now stood in silence, shrinking under fluorescent lights in a cold laboratory far from home.

I missed everything—my mother's quiet presence, my younger sister's laughter, the familiar rhythms of speaking Bengali, and the comfort of food that tasted like love.

But I could not share these struggles with my family, especially not with my mother, who was already worried and carrying the weight of a promise she had made to my father. I told her I was fine. That I was adjusting. That I was strong.

And in time, I became just that. But in those early days, I carried the loneliness like a secret, hidden behind smiles and polite nods, waiting for the moment when the walls would begin to crumble and friendship could find its way in. I missed home desperately.

Despite the isolation, I felt a sense of pride in what I was doing. No one in my family had ever traveled this far for education. I was doing something revolutionary, something that could change the trajectory of my life and inspire others to follow. This was my chance to prove not just to my family but to myself that I could rise above the obstacles in my path.

However, the promise I had made—always to make the right choices and never to tarnish the family name—was a constant weight on my shoulders. Each night, I put on a brave face, carefully managing every discussion so that my parents wouldn't worry. One evening, a few days after the lab incident, I called home just before dinner. My mother answered, her voice filled with relief and warmth.

"You're doing well, aren't you, dear?" my mom said. I took a breath, forcing a smile that she couldn't see. I replied, "Yes, everything's fine."

She paused. "You sound a little tired."

I laughed lightly. "Just a long day. We had a lab and a lecture back to back. I think I'll get used to the schedule soon."

From the background, my dad's voice came through faintly: "Ask her if she's eating well." My mom relayed it with gentle insistence. "And your meals? You're eating properly, right?"

I hesitated for half a second. The truth was, I had barely eaten anything that day. The spices in the food made my stomach churn, and my homesickness left little appetite. But I said, "Oh yes, the food is different, but I'm adjusting. I even tried something new today—vada pav!" I forced a cheerful tone.

She laughed. "That's my brave girl. Dad will be happy to hear that."

"Tell Dad not to worry," I said quickly. "I'm strong. I'll make you both proud."

After we hung up, I sat in the silence of the shared dorm room, staring at the unfamiliar ceiling. I missed home with an ache I didn't have words for. But I knew they needed to believe I was okay. So I became okay—one smile, one brave call at a time. I knew the stakes were high, and I had promised to uphold my family's honor. I could not falter.

Despite my determination, loneliness crept in, and doubt began to seep into my mind. I would lie awake at night, wondering if I had made a huge mistake.

As a young person, a minor—coming from a protected environment, it was challenging to navigate the complexities of life, sometimes unsure of what was right or wrong, but I knew I had to stand firm. I could not afford to make mistakes or fall into the wrong crowds. Each decision felt monumental, and I was walking this tightrope alone, far from home, with my mother silently bearing the burden of her own worries. I often found myself feeling like an outsider, asking, How do

I adapt? How can I overcome these challenges? Am I strong enough to face this alone?

One such moment is etched in my memory.

It was the week of Ganesh Chaturthi, a major celebration in Maharashtra (the state where Pune is located). The dorm's common room was buzzing with excitement. Girls were decorating the space with marigold garlands, setting up the idol of Lord Ganesha, practicing traditional songs and dances. The air smelled of incense, fried sweets, and joy.

But for me, it felt like another reminder of how far from home I was.

Back in Bengal, around this time, we would be preparing for Durga Puja—days filled with community pandals, dhak beats, and my mother's homemade sandesh (a delicious dessert made of milk and jaggery). The contrast was jarring. I didn't know about the Ganesh aarti (prayers). I didn't know the steps to their folk dance. When they handed out traditional attire to wear for the celebration, I hesitated.

One of the girls, well-meaning but unaware, said, "You probably don't get this festival much, right? It's a Maharashtrian thing." She smiled politely and turned back to her group.

She wasn't being unkind, but in that moment, I felt like a spectator in someone else's world. Not excluded, just irrelevant. I went back to my room and sat on the bed, hugging my knees. I didn't cry. I just sat there, quietly letting the feeling pass.

That night, I journaled like I always did. And at the bottom of the page, I wrote: "One day, I will belong—not because I fit in, but because I refuse to walk away."

It wasn't a declaration of victory. It was a promise to myself. A reminder that even if I felt like an outsider today, I was carving a place for myself, one act of courage at a time.

I was far from the comforts of home, but I knew I had to find a way to make this new environment my own. To answer these questions, I adopted what I now refer to as a "landscape assessment" approach. I took a deliberate step back to observe everything—my surroundings, the people, their cultural customs, their mannerisms, and their way of life. I studied my teachers, mentors, dorm mates, and classmates closely, not just to understand them but to gain an insight into their unique perspectives on life. I took note of how they interacted, how they celebrated their festivals, and how they navigated their daily challenges.

Initially, I was an anomaly to my peers—a girl from Bengal with a name, culture, and way of life that was unfamiliar. They weren't sure how to treat me or what to expect, and I didn't quite know how to fit in, either. Still, I persisted, and we warmed up to each other. Despite not speaking the language fluently, I found comfort in the kindness of the people around me. Their gestures of friendship, their smiles, and their willingness to include me in conversations eventually made me feel welcomed. I began to connect with them on a deeper level.

One evening, about three months into the school year, I found myself sitting in the common study hall of our all-women's dormitory, struggling to untangle a particularly complex section of my biochemistry project. The concepts blurred together, and no matter how many times I re-read the material, I couldn't make sense of it. I was used to figuring things out on my own, but that night, frustration quietly crept in.

Across the room sat a quiet girl named Anuja. She was known for keeping to herself, always focused, rarely speaking unless spoken to. That evening, however, she glanced up, noticed the tension on my face, and, to my surprise, walked over to me for the first time. "Are you stuck?" she asked gently. "Want to come with me for samosas and tea? I'm starving."

Her unexpected invitation caught me off guard, but I nodded, grateful for the kindness.

As we walked to the cafeteria and began talking, we quickly realized how different we were—our backgrounds, our routines, even our taste in food. Yet, over shared snacks and bursts of laughter, those differences slowly dissolved. For the first time since arriving, I felt a genuine sense of connection. What began as a simple, spontaneous invitation turned into the beginning of a meaningful friendship.

Later that week, Anuja surprised me with a small container of laddoos, an Indian dessert her mother had sent from home. "I thought you might like to try something different," she said, her voice laced with warmth. I smiled and offered her some chocolates I had tucked away. We didn't say much at that moment, but the silent exchange spoke volumes about kindness, belonging, and care.

That quiet act of reaching out to share a meal and some conversation marked a turning point. It reminded me that genuine connection doesn't always begin with dramatic gestures. Sometimes, it's tea and samosas. Sometimes, it's simply someone noticing you at just the right moment.

From then on, Anuja and I shared our dinners almost every night, talking about our classes, our families, our dreams, and our worries. She had her circle of friends, but with me, she became something special—a confidante, a cultural guide, a steady presence. Patiently, she introduced me to Marathi, the language spoken in this part of India. She helped me form simple sentences, encouraging me to communicate and engage with others more confidently in Marathi. In return, I shared my strategies for studying, helping her grasp complex concepts with greater ease.

Together, we helped each other grow, filling in one another's gaps with trust, curiosity, and compassion. What began as an unexpected gesture of friendship evolved into a space of shared learning, quiet resilience, and deep understanding. And in that space, I didn't just find my voice; I found a friend for life.

As time went on, I realized that the key to connecting with my peers wasn't about changing who I was; it was about meeting them halfway. The bridges we needed to build weren't made of shared backgrounds, but of shared effort. I came to understand that true connection grows not just through grand gestures, but through quiet moments of patience, curiosity, and empathy.

In those early days, I truly learned the power of observation. I watched how they laughed, how they teased each other, how they expressed care in ways that weren't always verbal. I noticed how a raised eyebrow could mean surprise, how a certain silence meant agreement, how certain slang words—foreign to my ears—carried layers of meaning. I paid attention to what made them feel seen and heard.

I also began to realize that language isn't just about vocabulary or dialect. It's about rhythm, timing, and intention. I had to learn to speak their language, not only literally, but emotionally. I began picking up bits of Marathi here and there, not just to blend in, but to show respect. I asked questions about their customs and festivals, and when they saw that I wasn't trying to impose my world onto them, but rather showing a genuine interest in theirs, something shifted.

Slowly, through genuine efforts to contribute and get involved, I started to earn the respect of the other students. I actively participated in class, collaborated with them on group projects, and encouraged teamwork whenever possible. I was always curious, eager to learn, and willing to help others with their work. This attitude didn't go unnoticed, especially by my teachers and mentors. They appreciated my approach to learning and my willingness to assist my classmates, and that recognition drove me to push myself even harder to excel academically.

It took about six months for my classmates to pronounce my name correctly. At first, they struggled, but their determination to get it right showed me that they were willing to make the effort. It was a small but significant milestone, the point when I felt I was no longer just a stranger in their eyes.

As I grew closer to my classmates, I noticed subtle shifts in their behavior. Some of them began bringing homemade food to share, a simple gesture that spoke volumes about the trust and affection they were starting to feel. Others in my dormitory began adopting some of my habits—the focus, discipline, and hard work that I demonstrated in our studies. Slowly but surely, the dormitory, once a noisy, bustling place filled with distractions, transformed into a quiet, focused space for collaboration, studying, and academic growth.

I felt proud of this shift, knowing that I had played a part in inspiring my peers to direct their energies into their studies and to make the most of the opportunities they had been given. Many of them, especially those from more traditional backgrounds, began to realize the value of channeling their efforts into their education, knowing that their families had made significant sacrifices to bring them to this point.

The parents, too, took notice of the positive impact I had on their daughters, who were my dorm mates. Over time, they saw that I wasn't just an outsider trying to fit in. I had become an integral part of their community. They appreciated the ways I helped their daughters navigate academic and personal challenges, and many of them came to me for advice, knowing that I had their children's best interests at heart. I had gone beyond being a classmate or a friend; I had become a mentor to many, guiding them through tough times and encouraging them to push their limits. They, in turn, began to accept me as part of their extended family, and this mutual respect became a foundation upon which I built lasting relationships.

This experience wasn't without its challenges. There were moments when I questioned my place in this new world. But it taught me the value of resilience and determination. By embracing the culture, learning the language, and celebrating their festivals with authenticity, I was able to slowly but surely earn the trust and affection of the people around me. What initially seemed like an impossible task—adapting to a completely new environment—transformed into an opportunity to build strong, meaningful relationships. I was no longer an outsider but a well-integrated part of this new world.

Despite the emotional toll, I felt empowered by being the first in my family to step out, defy the norms, and challenge the limitations that were imposed on women in my community. Every attempt I made to rise above these difficulties was a small act of defiance against the odds. This was my chance to bring about change, to show that with determination and courage, anything was possible. It wasn't easy, but it was worth every struggle. This journey, though difficult, had the power to reshape not only my future but the future of those who would follow in my footsteps. With that thought, I found the strength to keep moving forward.

I can now see how this journey shaped who I am today. The lessons I learned in those early days—the importance of patience, persistence, and understanding—continue to influence my approach to life and work. It wasn't just about fitting in; it was about contributing, respecting differences, and creating a space where we could all grow together. This journey, with all its challenges and rewards, remains one of the most significant chapters of my life.

My life in Pune had settled into a rhythm. I had built lasting friendships, forged valuable mentorships, and excelled academically. At the same time, the ambition to continue my education at a global level began to stir within me. I was dreaming of pursuing a PhD in the United States, a leap that felt like the natural next step in my journey.

At the time, I was deeply immersed in writing my research thesis in microbiology and had already published several research papers in prestigious international journals. The foundation of my dream was solid. I had worked tirelessly, focused on achieving excellence, turning challenges into opportunities, and nurturing my ambitions. With these habits, I felt ready to take the next step. I decided to pursue higher education in the United States, with the goal of expanding my academic growth. I applied for scholarships to multiple PhD programs in cancer research that aligned with the trajectory I wanted to take in the oncology field.

In March, an unexpected phone call came. I had been busy with exam preparation all day, completely unaware that my parents had been trying to reach me. When I returned to my dorm, the phone rang almost immediately. I could sense that something was different. My father's voice, usually calm and collected, was laced with frustration. "Where have you been? I've been trying to call you all day," he said.

"I've been studying at the library. What's wrong?" I responded. What he told me next took me completely by surprise.

"Do you know that you've been selected for a PhD program with a full scholarship to study at North Dakota State University in America?" he said in a rush, almost exasperated.

My initial reaction was disbelief about the news itself and the fact that he was so annoyed. "Dad, this is amazing! Why are you upset?" I asked.

His tone shifted to overwhelming pride as he explained, "I was just so excited to tell you, and you weren't answering the phone! I'm so proud of you."

This was the moment I realized how far I had come. My father, who had once opposed my desire to move to Pune for further studies, was now my biggest cheerleader. He was genuinely proud and deeply moved by my success. It felt like a full-circle moment of transformation.

My father was now living out one of his dreams through me. My dad had once been offered opportunities to study in Canada and Germany, but due to his responsibilities as the only son, his parents had prevented him from going. Now, I was going to travel six thousand miles to fulfill the dreams he could not. It was a triumph for both of us—a family moment of pride and joy—and this time, my entire family stood by me, supporting me unconditionally. They were all my champions.

This moment was a turning point, both for me and my relationship with my father. I had won him over, not through persuasion or convincing words but through my actions, dedication, and achievements. My performance in Pune had shown him that I was ready to take on the world.

With a full scholarship covering the entirety of my PhD program, I had not only earned an academic honor; I had been granted a profound opportunity: to prove my worth on a global stage and to etch my mark upon the world. It was more than recognition; it was a passport to possibility, a quiet affirmation that my voice, my vision, and my work belong in the rooms where people are making impacts and shaping futures. As a girl, I was the first in my family to earn such a distinction—a testament to my resilience, hard work, and determination. It felt incredibly satisfying to see how my journey had impacted not only my life but also the lives of my family members, as they watched me achieve what had once seemed impossible.

In that instant, I also realized the power of resilience. I not only overcame challenges in my academic life, but I also bridged cultural and familial divides. I had learned to adapt to the way of life in Pune, celebrating their festivals, learning their language, and truly becoming a part of their community. By respecting and immersing myself in their culture, I had built deep connections with my friends, mentors, and even dorm mates. There were no ulterior motives—just a genuine desire to understand them and for them to understand me in return.

Looking back, I've come to recognize just how vital it is not only to assess one's environment but also to adapt to it with intention and grace. Among the many strategies I've encountered, it was the simple yet transformative act of cultural immersion that proved to be the cornerstone of my personal and academic journey. I ventured forth with no agenda beyond the desire to learn, to grow, and to embrace each experience with humility and openness.

Whether I found myself navigating the vibrant rhythms of Pune or adjusting to unfamiliar corners of the world, I met every challenge with a curious spirit and a genuine willingness to understand the people, customs, and values around me. In doing so, I didn't just achieve academic success; I cultivated a deep sense of belonging, self-assurance, and the courage to transcend limitations imposed by convention or expectation.

This journey taught me that the road to personal growth is rarely linear. It is filled with detours, setbacks, and unexpected lessons. But through persistence and an unwavering belief in oneself, what once seemed like insurmountable obstacles gradually transformed into stepping stones. I came to see myself like water—fluid yet determined—able to navigate around barriers, never losing momentum, always finding a path forward.

In essence, this experience reaffirmed a profound truth: that nothing is truly impossible when one remains resilient, open-hearted, and steadfast in pursuit of one's dreams. It is in embracing both the challenge and the change that we discover our true capacity to evolve—and to thrive.

My message to all women and girls who feel trapped by cultural limitations: When you step into a new place, take a moment to observe, listen, and embrace the world around you. While staying true to your own identity, allow yourself to blend in with the culture, adapt to the local food, and connect with the people. Open your heart to new friendships, for it is through kindness and humility that you will form bonds. Leave your ego behind and extend warmth to others; they will do the same in return. Together, you will grow, learn, and thrive. After all, when in Rome, do as the Romans do.

CHAPTER 4

From India to America: A Journey of Resilience, Purpose, and Triumph

When I received the news that I would be going to the U.S. to pursue advanced studies and fulfill my American dream, my excitement was palpable. This time around, my parents and extended family were in awe, stunned yet exhilarated by my achievement.

My mother and father were immensely proud because no one on either side of our family had ever accomplished this before—the opportunity not only for advanced studies but to do so in the U.S. My father's pride was further magnified by the fact that none of his friends' or colleagues' children had yet obtained such an opportunity. While I found his measure of success somewhat superficial at the time, securing a full scholarship to study in America was a rarity, garnering immense prestige in our community.

As my departure neared, my mother posed a question to me that made me pause: "Are you not afraid to leave your family behind? To venture so far away, to another continent six thousand miles from home?" I think in all the hustle and bustle, she hadn't realized the ramifications of my studying in America. It finally dawned on her as we were packing my bags. This was a moment of truth for her: "Oh, my God. My child is moving six thousand miles away. Who knows when I'll see her again?"

Her question took me by surprise and made me pause as well. I had been so busy running along, making my parents happy, fulfilling their dreams and mine, that I'd never stopped to ask myself how I felt about everything. However, without even thinking about it, I met her gaze and replied with quiet determination, "No, I will manage." This was a spontaneous response. Then, with solemn conviction, I added, "I promise, Mom, I will never let our family name be tarnished."

I knew what we had gone through to convince my dad to let me go to Pune for higher studies. This time around, there was an overwhelming sense of happiness, but the fact remained in our minds that whenever a girl was leaving home, she had to promise to uphold the family name. So, I did.

With that promise, I embarked on my journey to chase the American dream. My parents filled my suitcases with rice, lentils, new clothes, and an assortment of essentials they had lovingly gathered. When you're leaving behind the people you love, your culture, and your comfort food, it creates a sense of displacement. My parents knew that packing the foods that I love would feel like bringing a piece of home with me to America. My parents had done so much for me, and I was grateful. When the moment arrived, with tear-filled eyes, we embraced, and I bid farewell to India.

This was huge for me, as I was embarking on my first international journey. As I boarded that flight, I silently vowed to nurture and elevate myself, to make my parents swell with pride. I would carry our family's name with honor. I have always been grateful that my parents gave me the wings to fly, especially as a girl at a time when such opportunities were far from common in our society. I felt a lot of pride and gratitude for my parents and what they had done as I bid farewell to India and left my motherland.

I arrived in Fargo, North Dakota, ready to begin my PhD in biochemistry with a focus on oncology. I felt euphoric as I stepped into this new world. Yes, I felt sad about leaving my family behind, but the moment I reached Fargo, I thought, I have my wings. I'm embarking on an independent life in a new country, with new people, and I am going to live my American dream. The pain of leaving my family behind was mixed with a sense of achievement and happiness.

It was July, and the warmth of summer was matched by the welcome I received at the airport. People from my lab were there to greet me, and in that moment, I felt triumphant, as if I had won an Oscar. Silly me.

Reality quickly kicked in. I was completely caught up in the whirlwind of my new life when I remembered I needed to call my parents. There was no phone booth at the airport, so I had no way to immediately call them. They stayed awake all night, anxiously awaiting my voice. Eventually, I managed to reach them, and only after hearing that I had arrived safely did they allow themselves to rest.

Looking back now, I realize how much courage and trust it took for them to let me go. Sending their daughter alone into an unknown country across the world without any precedent in our family was a huge deal. It's likely easier for parents nowadays, but at that time, when none of us had ever done or even heard of anyone doing anything like this, it required a huge amount of belief in me for them to let their little girl go.

I soon settled into my new life. I lived in a two-bedroom apartment, with a kitchen and a small living room, which I shared with an apartment mate. I spent my days in a research lab and attending classes. The promise of the future I had dreamed of was staring me in the face. At first, everything felt exhilarating, but soon, reality caught up with me. The independence I had longed for came with unexpected challenges.

I was working long hours in the lab, studying for my classes, cooking my own meals, returning to an empty apartment, washing dishes, paying bills, and cleaning. Suddenly, adulthood was no longer just an abstract concept. It was my daily life, and I was utterly unprepared. There was no running to my parents for comfort or guidance. Every decision, every struggle, was mine alone to navigate.

The cultural shock was profound. Though my time in Pune had prepared me in some ways, nothing could have fully braced me for this. My neighbors kept to themselves, and for the first time, I felt truly lonely. I put on a cheerful front at the lab, laughing with friends, but inside, I was struggling. The time difference made it difficult to speak to my parents as often as I wished, and that ache of separation weighed on me. I felt as if I had been ripped away from the warm cocoon of my family.

Even the simplest things—like cooking—became battles. For the first three months, I burned meals, went hungry, or survived on take-out burritos. Some nights, as I struggled over the stove, tears would well up in my eyes. It was in those moments that I truly grasped what it meant to be alone in America.

I recall one night when loneliness struck me particularly hard. I had been working late in the lab, immersed in experiments and deadlines, paying little attention to the world outside. I hadn't seen the weather alerts about the blizzard we were expecting. By the time I stepped outside, convinced I could make the short fifteen-minute walk home, the campus had transformed into a white sea. Snow covered everything—cars, sidewalks, signs—and the wind howled through the empty streets like a warning I hadn't heeded.

At first, I thought it was just a little storm. But within minutes, the cold became unbearable. The wind slapped against my face, stinging my skin and stealing my breath. Snowdrifts rose around my boots with every step, and soon I realized that I was out in this mess completely alone. On other nights, I'd see students heading home, backpacks slung over their shoulders, chatting in small groups. But tonight, not a soul was in sight.

The silence was eerie. The roads had vanished. The world had gone still, save for the howling wind. I pressed forward, each step more difficult than the last, praying I wouldn't fall or lose my way.

When I finally reached my apartment, shivering and soaked, I collapsed onto the floor. My fingers trembled as I turned on the television, and there it was: Severe Blizzard Warning. Residents are advised to stay indoors due to the risk of frostbite. Travel is highly discouraged.

I had walked through a blizzard. And in that moment, the reality hit me that I could have died out there, alone, in a foreign country. No one would have known.

That night, I missed my mother's soft hand on my head, her instinct to check the skies before I stepped outside. I missed the familiar chaos of the dorm in Pune—the echo of neighbors' voices, the hum of a radio playing an old Bollywood song, the smell of pakoras sizzling in a nearby home. Here, even silence felt unfamiliar. Sharp, cold, and distant.

I tried calling my parents. The connection was poor. My father's voice crackled, "Hello? Hello?" My mother's image froze mid-smile on the screen. We gave up after a few moments of static and silence.

That night, I curled up in bed, still wearing my coat, and let the tears come. For the first time in years, I cried myself to sleep. Not out of weakness, but because the weight of solitude had finally settled in. It was the night I truly understood what it meant to be alone in America.

Despite the difficulties, I adapted, slowly but surely, just as I had in Pune. I made genuine efforts to connect with my peers. I shared parts of myself, stories about my life, and I asked questions about their cultures. I learned to cook from the friends I met at graduate school and in my apartment complex. I built routines. I found my resilience.

Amidst the struggles, I reminded myself why I had come to America: to build something meaningful, to make my family proud, and to honor the faith that they had placed in me. My American journey had begun.

As life gradually settled into a rhythm, my days revolved around long hours in the lab, exam preparation, and the occasional outing with friends. Then came Christmas Eve, an evening that would change my life in ways I never anticipated.

My apartment mate, Diya, invited me to a Christmas dinner at her friend's house. Having studied in a convent school, Christmas has always been a familiar and joyous occasion, so I was thrilled at the prospect of attending a church service and celebrating with friends. The hosts were a couple in their 50s, Joe and Elizabeth. The woman, graceful and warm, welcomed us with open arms. The moment I stepped into their home, I felt something I hadn't in a long time: comfort, belonging, a sense of home. Her kindness and hospitality melted away the lingering loneliness and restlessness within me.

From that night on, their home became my place of comfort, and Elizabeth became one of my best friends. Every special occasion was spent with them, sharing laughter over hearty meals of salads, pasta, and lasagna, savoring decadent desserts, and basking in the warmth of their presence. We became a family, and for the first time in America, my heart felt full.

But the unthinkable happened. One day, Joe broke the news with a somber face. Elizabeth had been diagnosed with breast cancer. The woman who had been my anchor, so full of life and love, was now facing a battle that threatened to take it all away. As she underwent rounds of chemotherapy and surgeries, I watched her transformation helplessly: her vibrant spirit faded, her body grew weaker, and a haunting frailty overshadowed her radiant smile.

The first time I saw her after treatment, the shock was overwhelming. Her hair was gone. Her once lively eyes had dulled, and her body was weak. Until then, cancer had just been a subject of my research, a distant, abstract enemy. But now it had a face and a name, and it had struck someone I loved. The weight of this realization consumed me. She was never far from my thoughts. Even as I buried myself in my work, conducting experiments and writing papers, I found myself thinking about her.

That was the moment I pledged to devote my life to cancer research. Fueled by newfound purpose, I pushed my limits, working tirelessly to excel in my field. Remember, I said my name means "one who is devoted to a mission." This was my second mission: to do something for cancer patients and to pledge my life to cancer research. I poured my heart into publishing papers, writing my thesis, and striving to make a meaningful impact through my work.

Over time, Elizabeth began to recover, slowly regaining her strength, though she was never quite the same. Despite everything, she remained a source of light in my life. By then, I had moved into a small one-bedroom apartment, and she lovingly helped me turn that space into a home. Though solitude often lingered in the corners of my life, there was peace in knowing I was on the path I was meant to walk on.

Years passed, and the day finally arrived: my doctoral dissertation defense. Elizabeth stood by my side, just as I stood by hers. She beamed with joy, bringing cakes, balloons, and celebrations for all who attended my dissertation defense meeting. Thanks to her prayers, the unwavering support of my parents, and my relentless hard work, I defended my thesis with confidence and ease. The journey had been long, but it had led me here, to this moment of triumph.

I graduated with a PhD in biochemistry, with a specialization in oncology. I even had ten published original scientific articles bearing my name. In recognition of my academic excellence, I was honored with the Global Outreach Ambassador Award for two consecutive years and the Green and Golden Globe Diversity Award from North Dakota State University.

Earning my PhD and receiving the title of "doctor" marked a profound and deeply personal milestone—one that had never before been achieved within my family or local community back home. It was more than an academic honor; it was a symbol of possibility, perseverance, and a quiet defiance against limitations long accepted as norms.

Thousands of miles away in India, my family overflowed with pride and joy. Their excitement knew no bounds; they could hardly sleep the night before my graduation, their hearts brimming with emotion even across oceans and time zones. Though distance separated us physically, their presence was palpable. They found every way they could to share in my moment, their voices on the phone bridging continents, filling the room with love and celebration. In that moment, my two worlds—my biological family and the chosen family I had built through friendship and shared experience—came together in perfect harmony.

There was, indeed, so much to celebrate. I had plunged headfirst into rigorous academic challenges and daunting life transitions, and I didn't merely endure—I thrived. Each obstacle met with fierce determination, each long night softened by the encouragement of those who believed in me, helped shape the resilient person I had become. I reached for my dreams, and in doing so, I found not only professional success but also deep personal growth and lasting relationships that enriched my journey.

In achieving what once felt distant, I came to understand the true weight and worth of meaningful accomplishments. I was still young, but already I had discovered the empowering sense of purpose that comes from setting your sights high and chasing those aspirations with unwavering resolve.

As I stood at that turning point, diploma in hand, I knew I was ready for the next chapter. The road ahead was uncharted, its turns and triumphs yet to be revealed. But I no longer feared the unknown. I welcomed it with open arms, a full heart, and a spirit fueled by dreams still unfolding and a life yet to be written.

> **My message to all the girls who are willing to embark on a new life journey:** No dream is too big, and no challenge is too great when fueled by resilience and a sense of purpose. Stepping into the unknown may feel overwhelming, but with perseverance, adoption, adaptation, and the right support, you will find your way. Every struggle is an opportunity to grow, and every setback can ignite a new purpose. Stay committed, embrace change, and let your journey be a testament to the power of determination and hope.

CHAPTER 5

New Beginnings in New Jersey: A Bold Leap Balancing Love, Career, and the Pursuit of Purpose

Amid the pressures of completing my thesis and preparing for my doctoral defense, love quietly found its way into my life. Shrikant and I met through mutual friends during my early graduate days in the U.S. What began as casual conversations over the phone slowly deepened into a bond that stayed strong over the years. We navigated a long-distance relationship with patience and quiet understanding. While I focused on making my parents proud and achieving my goals, he stood by me, unwavering in his support. My parents didn't know the whole story then. I guarded that part of my life, knowing the timing had to be right.

So, when Shrikant proposed, I said "yes" without hesitation—and perhaps most boldly, without even asking my parents. It was a courageous decision. In India, marriages outside one's community often face resistance, and ours was no exception. When we finally broke the news to our families, both sides were taken aback. It may seem natural to some, but in India, not asking your parents for permission is quite unusual. I am from East India, and he is from South India; although our communities are different, the approach to marriage is similar.

In Western culture, it's normal to find your partner, fall in love, decide together on marriage, and then for the man to ask for the woman's hand from her father. In Indian culture, however, the couple does not decide on their own. Decisions about marriage happen with the involvement and consent of both families. It's not an individualistic community; it's a very family-oriented community. It was a courageous and bold move when I said "yes" to Shrikant's proposal. I knew in my gut that I loved him, and I had faith that it would work out. It took persistent persuasion, deep conversations, and unwavering belief in our bond to gain the approval of both our families.

By this point, my parents had come to accept that I was someone who walked uncharted paths, a torch-bearer of change within the family. Still, I was breaking tradition, and they worried about how the world and their friends and family would react. I didn't blame them. Their response stemmed from the environment they grew up in. Societal norms had conditioned them, and they did not know any better. But I have always trusted my instincts, and this time was no exception.

Our wedding in India was nothing short of a vibrant celebration—an unforgettable chapter woven with love, tradition, and joy. Approximately five hundred people gathered to witness this special moment, and in true Indian fashion, the festivities spanned five vibrant days. What made it even more extraordinary was not just the number of attendees, but their unwavering presence; every single guest enjoyed the activities, fully immersed in the rituals, laughter, and togetherness that only an Indian wedding can offer.

It felt like a double celebration—a perfect confluence of two monumental milestones. I had just earned my PhD, a moment of immense personal and academic triumph, and now I was preparing to marry the love of my life. The air was thick with emotion and festivity, filled with music, colors, sacred vows, and the warmth of those who had supported me throughout my journey.

To be surrounded by family and friends at such a pivotal moment—standing at the intersection of achievement and new beginnings—was profoundly moving. The days were long, but they passed in a joyful blur of tradition and heartfelt blessings. Each ritual felt deeper, each smile more meaningful, because it wasn't just a union of two people; it was the celebration of perseverance, love, and the beautiful merging of lives and legacies.

In every way, it was a culmination of dreams realized and a future embraced, and I will forever carry the memory of those five glorious days, where the celebration of my academic journey seamlessly became the celebration of our shared life ahead.

As I stood amidst the celebration, I felt the weight and wonder of countless eyes upon me, not with judgment, but with admiration, hope, and pride. I could see it clearly in their expressions: mothers wishing the same career path for their daughters, young girls seeing a reflection of what was possible, and women quietly cheering for a future that looked a little more like their dreams. It was a deeply moving moment. In their gaze, I realized that I was more than a graduate or a bride—I had become a symbol of aspiration, strength, and change.

The congratulations came in waves, heartfelt and abundant. I was being honored not just for becoming a doctor, but also for embracing love on my own terms—marrying outside of my community, a step that no one in my family had ever taken. The cultural expectations we had lived under were strong, and my mother, though proud, carried quiet fears about how society would perceive our decision. I knew those fears were not unfounded; they were the echoes of generations of caution and conformity.

And yet, during those five remarkable days, something beautiful unfolded. The people who came to celebrate us embraced my husband with open hearts. Their kindness and acceptance gently dissolved the apprehensions my parents had held onto. Their warmth and encouragement soothed old worries, offering a kind of validation that words alone could never provide.

It felt extraordinary—liberating, even. I stood tall with a profound sense of pride, knowing that once again, with the steady support of my parents, I had defied expectations and redefined what was possible. I know it wasn't always easy for them to walk this unconventional path with me, but they did—with love, courage, and grace. Together, we had broken yet another mold, reshaped another tradition, and embraced a future we authored ourselves.

In that moment, surrounded by love, acceptance, and new beginnings, I felt a deep sense of completion. I had come full circle, carrying forward the values of my upbringing while boldly carving a new legacy.

And in doing so, I offered others not just a glimpse of what could be, but permission to dream beyond boundaries.

The excitement of settling into our first home together was immeasurable. No longer alone, I reveled in the joys of companionship, cooking together, sharing simple moments, and nurturing our new life as husband and wife. However, the urgent need to secure my immigration status interrupted the bliss of our newly married life. We had barely begun building a life together when reality came knocking—visa timelines, paperwork, and the constant fear of uncertainty. I needed to find a job quickly, not just to support us, but to stay in the country legally.

In between setting up our first home in New Jersey—figuring out grocery lists, laughing over burnt dinners, and learning how to be husband and wife—I was also sending out resumes, navigating interviews, and praying for a breakthrough. The joy of companionship softened the edges of this stressful period, but the pressure was real.

After numerous rounds of discussions, technical evaluations, and presentations, I was fortunate to receive offers from two leading oncology research centers in New Jersey. After much deliberation, I chose to join a renowned comprehensive cancer center as a Pediatric Oncology Scientist. This position allowed me to stabilize my immigration status.

In this role, I was honored with the Young Investigator Award and received a one-hundred-thousand-dollar grant for hematology-oncology research. It was a moment of immense pride, not just for me but for my entire family. My parents were thrilled, yet understandably, their focus had shifted to the immediate responsibilities of my other siblings and their own lives. "Out of sight, out of mind" was perhaps an inevitability for me, considering the size of our family.

In their place, however, I found another unwavering pillar of support in Shrikant. He stepped into the role my parents had once played, becoming my greatest cheerleader, standing beside me as I received the award. He has stood beside me at this pivotal moment in my life, and I have been mindful of nurturing my relationships so that the people I love and care for are there for me, and I am there for them.

Starting a new role in a new city with new responsibilities came with its own set of challenges. The initial days were overwhelming, as I had to manage a new home with a husband, prove myself at work, and meet the high expectations that came with the position. There were moments of solitude and silent tears.

But I pushed forward. My days were consumed with research, conducting experiments, collaborating with my team, attending lab meetings, and even sitting in on tumor boards to discuss patient treatment regimens with accomplished physicians, surgeons, and researchers. The weight of challenging experiments, grant proposals, and manuscript writing was immense.

At home, I juggled my responsibilities as a wife and homemaker, nurturing our marriage while navigating the complexities of a demanding profession. Despite Shrikant's unwavering support, the relentless pursuit of excellence in my professional and personal life left me drained. The pressure to meet expectations, both my own and those of the world around me, was relentless.

I remember one winter morning in particular. I had an important presentation at the cancer center on my recent research findings. I woke up at 4:30 a.m., careful not to wake Shrikant as I slipped into the next room, still in my pajamas, hair pulled into a messy bun. I finished my thorough review of the deck just as the sun came up, and before I could catch my breath, I rushed into the kitchen to pack lunch, prepare tea, and review the grocery list. By 8:00 a.m., I was out the door, heels on, a smile fixed in place for a full day of work.

At the hospital, I delivered the new research presentation, fielded a flurry of emails, and stayed late to work with a colleague on a time-sensitive deliverable. On the way home, I stopped at the store, picked up vegetables, and walked into our apartment, already mentally preparing what to cook for dinner. By the time I finished the dishes and wiped down the kitchen counters, it was past 11 p.m. Shrikant, ever patient, asked me to sit down and take a breath, but I just smiled and said, "Almost done."

When I finally crawled into bed, exhausted and aching, I cried softly into my pillow—not out of regret, but because I was simply tired. I was doing it all. And I was doing it alone, even with all the love in the world beside me. Still, I woke up the next morning and did it all over again.

The words of Indra Nooyi—an Indian-born American business executive who was the chairman and CEO of PepsiCo for thirteen years—echoed in my mind: "A woman can't have it all." Maybe a woman can have it all, but at what cost? The cost is very high. I soon realized that "having it all" meant climbing an exhausting uphill battle every single day. Indra was speaking for all ambitious working mothers. Her generation, my generation, every new generation of ferocious, go-getter women—we are speaking out. We are proclaiming loudly that we can't have it all, while in our hearts, we are craving, shouting, and wishing that we could, just like men.

So, what will we tell the next generation of women? Will we continue to echo the refrain that we can't have it all? Or will we reframe the narrative—one built not on limitations, but on possibilities shaped by intention, resilience, and sacrifice?

The truth is, if you are driven by purpose and fueled by a desire to succeed, you cannot wait for opportunities to be handed to you. Life rarely offers anything on a silver platter. You must carve out your own path, even when it's steep and uncertain. You must build the scaffolding that will support your ambitions by creating your own opportunities, cultivating meaningful relationships, and fostering systems of support that grow with you, not in spite of you.

But let us not romanticize this journey. The pursuit of "having it all"—a fulfilling career, a loving family, personal peace, and societal impact—comes at a price. It demands relentless commitment, difficult trade-offs, and a willingness to confront moments of doubt and exhaustion. It requires that those around you—partners, family, colleagues—carry the weight with you, not as spectators, but as active participants in your vision.

In sharing my story, I don't seek applause; I aim to shift the paradigm. I want young women to know that it is possible to have it all, but they must enter that pursuit with their eyes wide open. There will be sacrifices. There will be late nights, missed milestones, and choices that others may not understand. But there will also be pride, growth, and the quiet triumph of knowing you shaped your destiny with courage and conviction.

In navigating the delicate balance between my new roles—as an oncology scientist, a homemaker, and a wife—I uncovered a deeper truth about myself: I am not one to shy away from challenges. Instead, I meet them head-on, embracing each responsibility with both determination and grace. These roles, each demanding in their own right, did not deter me. They became opportunities—platforms upon which I could prove to myself that commitment, when guided by purpose, can transcend limitations.

I never waited for the perfect moment or the certainty of success. With every bold decision I made—whether in the laboratory, in shaping a home, or in nurturing a partnership—the outcome was uncertain. I didn't know whether I would thrive or falter, whether I would be celebrated or misunderstood. But what I did know was that I had within me the resolve to try, and the resourcefulness to adapt. I leaned on every tool I had gathered—strategies honed through experience, insights born from struggle, and a steady, fast belief that discipline and heart could carry me through.

There were no guarantees, no safety nets, just a quiet but unwavering promise to myself: to show up fully, to give my best, and to continue growing in the face of the unknown. It is in that space between uncertainty and courage that I found my strength. And in doing so, I reaffirmed that you don't have to sacrifice your career, your ambition, or your aspirations when you're willing to forge your own path with conviction, resilience, and grace.

As I took each small step, I understood that I was on a journey of self-discovery. Making a decision is one thing, but having the drive, power, and mental and emotional strength to follow through is entirely a different game. It takes great determination. When you decide to do something, you must follow through and do everything that's required to achieve that goal.

I watched myself grow as I set new goals. Each decision of mine became bolder and bolder as I grew braver and braver. And after several meaningful years in research, I realized I was ready for the next courageous step.

While my work as a researcher was deeply fulfilling, I found myself longing to make an even broader impact. My mentor and manager, an exceptional oncologist, dedicated his life to advancing cancer treatment. Inspired by his vision, I felt a calling to step beyond the lab bench, bridge the gap between science and business, and contribute to patient care on a much larger scale. I wanted to explore ways to improve patient outcomes.

With that conviction, I made a bold decision to transition from the research lab to the business side of medicine. I applied to the Marketing and Pharmaceutical Management Dual MBA Program at Rutgers Business School and, to my astonishment, was awarded a seventy percent scholarship. The realization that my path was evolving into something greater filled me with a sense of purpose.

Saying goodbye to my research career was bittersweet. During my tenure working at a comprehensive cancer center, I published two research papers and a review article, served on the editorial boards of four international journals, and reviewed manuscripts from over twenty-five oncology-focused scientific journals. I also led and contributed to an innovative research project, one that would continue beyond my departure.

As I bid farewell to the lab, I carried with me not only a wealth of scientific knowledge but also an unwavering commitment to advancing healthcare in innovative and transformative ways. With heartfelt gratitude and a vision for the future, I embarked on yet another remarkable journey, one where science and strategy would intersect, shaping the future of medicine and patient care.

Amid this transition, I would be lying if I said I wasn't afraid. I deeply and absolutely feared losing a part of my identity. For so long, I had poured my heart into scientific inquiry, building a life grounded in the rigor and rhythm of research. The laboratory had been both my sanctuary and my proving ground. Stepping away from it felt like letting go of a part of myself.

What made the shift even more daunting was the absence of a clear precedent. I had no blueprint, no mentor who had made this exact journey from the academic depths of scientific oncology research to the dynamic, fast-paced world of business. Had I seen someone else do it, perhaps I could have drawn confidence from their example—reassured myself with the thought: They did it, so I can too.

But there was no one I could turn to for guidance. I was stepping into uncharted territory. There were no guarantees, no promises of success, only questions: Would I thrive? Would I be accepted in a space that spoke a different language than the one I'd mastered? Would my scientific background be a strength or a barrier?

But sometimes, growth demands that we walk into the unknown with nothing but faith in ourselves. I took that leap, not because I was certain, but because I knew that remaining where I was, simply out of fear, would be a disservice to my potential. And though the future was uncertain, the courage to take that first step became the foundation for a new chapter—one that honored where I came from, while embracing who I was becoming.

One thing I know with absolute clarity is that I am strong-willed. I cherish that about myself. When I have a vision, I pursue it with unwavering determination. Once I set my sights on a goal, I commit fully, allowing neither doubt nor distraction to steer me away. That inner fire, that resolute focus, has been my compass through every stage of my journey.

I wear my successes not with arrogance, but with deep pride and abiding gratitude. I am fully aware that my path has been shaped not only by my own drive but also by the support, encouragement, and love I've received along the way. And yet, the journey has not been without its trials. I have encountered struggles—some visible, many invisible—that have tested my strength and demanded resilience. But I've never let them define me. Instead, I've let them refine me.

I'm someone who is constantly pushing boundaries—challenging myself to rise to new heights, to take on greater responsibilities, to grow in arenas that once felt daunting. Venturing into and succeeding within the complex and emotionally charged field of pediatric oncology is just one example of that inner calling to do more, to be more.

My achievements haven't followed a straight, predictable path. They've come in waves—sometimes crashing, sometimes calm, but always carrying me forward. Through it all, I continue to evolve, learning and transforming with each experience, each challenge, and each small triumph. I am, and always will be, a work in progress—growing, striving, and becoming the most authentic version of myself.

I found great success as an oncology scientist, but I've never defined success solely by professional accolades or academic accomplishments. For me, true success lies in how far you're willing to stretch yourself and how deeply you're compelled to become a conduit for meaningful change. It's about using your talents not just to advance your own career, but to elevate the lives of others, especially those who are vulnerable and in need. From the beginning, I was unwavering in my commitment to helping cancer patients. That singular purpose fueled my every endeavor.

It was this passion and a deep trust in my instincts that gave me the courage to take a leap of faith and pursue the next chapter of my journey: business school. I carried with me not only a scientific foundation but a strong sense of resilience and adaptability—qualities that I forged through years of navigating complex challenges in the lab and beyond. Even though I didn't yet know the outcome of this decision, I saw this path with remarkable clarity. It was less about certainty and more about conviction.

My vision was bold: to blend science, business, and advocacy into a unified force for good. I aspired to craft a career where I could influence the future of patient care, not from just one vantage point, but through a multifaceted, impactful lens that bridged science, strategy, and compassion. In a world where professionals often operate in silos—either deeply rooted in research or immersed in the commercial aspect of drug development—I sought to bridge the gap. I wanted to be the bridge between discovery and delivery, between data and impact, between knowledge and action.

This choice was not just about reinventing myself; it was about expanding the boundaries of what a purpose-driven life could look like. I wasn't leaving science behind—I was building upon it, with the hope of creating something even more powerful and transformative.

> **My message to the world:** Life's journey is shaped by bold choices, resilience, and the courage to break barriers. Balancing love, career, and ambition is never easy, but with perseverance and adaptability, growth becomes inevitable. Every challenge is an invitation to redefine purpose. Embrace change, trust your instincts, and never be afraid to carve your own path—for that is where true fulfillment begins.

CHAPTER 6

The Transformative Journey of Motherhood: Balancing Ambition, Love, and Self-Discovery

Before I invite you into the story of my transformative journey to business school, it is important to begin with a chapter that has quietly shaped every part of who I am: motherhood. This experience—rich with lessons, challenges, and moments of profound growth—has left an indelible mark on both my personal and professional life. It is through this lens that I made many of my choices, and the woman I have become truly emerged. Without understanding this part of my journey, the depth and meaning of what followed would remain incomplete.

My husband and I had built a life together that was both stable and deeply fulfilling—a life shaped by shared values, mutual respect, and an unspoken understanding of each other's ambitions. Together, we struck a delicate yet deliberate balance between our professional pursuits and our personal world, carving out space for connection, growth, and joy amidst the demands of high-pressure careers.

He held the role of Vice President of Global Technology at a leading Investment Bank, a position that demanded vision, agility, and relentless dedication. I, meanwhile, was fully immersed in my work as a Pediatric Oncology Scientist at one of New Jersey's most prestigious Comprehensive Cancer Centers, driven by purpose and the pursuit of progress in the fight against cancer. Though our careers were distinct in focus, they mirrored each other in intensity and in the deep sense of responsibility we each carried.

At the same time, we were navigating the complex and often exhausting journey of securing U.S. citizenship—a process filled with hope, uncertainty, and countless hurdles. It was not just a legal transition; it was a step toward truly belonging in the country we had come to call home, a country where we were contributing our talents and building our future.

Through it all, we leaned on each other—balancing ambition with love, structure with spontaneity, and determination with grace. What we built wasn't just a household; it was a partnership grounded in resilience and possibility, a testament to what two people can achieve when they move forward together, hand in hand.

In addition to all of that, we decided it was finally time to start a family. We didn't rush into this decision because I don't take on responsibility unless I'm ready for it. I weigh out the options. I consider my environment, my resources, and my strategies. When everything feels in place, then I execute. Shrikant and I had always planned to be parents, and we made the decision in our own time. We were at a point in our lives where the gentle yet persistent pressures of family nudged us toward parenthood, and we wanted to embrace this new chapter.

During this phase of my career, I was deeply immersed in my research, writing a paper, drafting a review article, and conducting experiments for another project. Determined to complete my commitments before maternity leave, I worked tirelessly until eight and a half months into my pregnancy. I'm very organized, planning things far in advance before executing them. I knew that if I was healthy and my doctor agreed, I could work until right before my daughter was born. As a professional, I have never viewed my work as merely a job. I'm passionate about it. I treat it like it's my baby because, from the age of four, when I started learning my ABCs, ever since I can remember, I aspired to become a doctor, and I've been pursuing that goal. My job is not a job. It's a legacy that I'm building.

Still, a quiet voice in my mind questioned my relentless pace: Why are you racing? Why do you need to prove yourself now? Nobody's judging you.

Yet, deep down, I wasn't sure. Perhaps people were judging me, or perhaps I had unknowingly internalized a belief that my worth was tethered to constant productivity. That slowing down—even for a moment—might be perceived as a weakness or a lack of ambition. I had trained myself to equate success with motion, measuring my progress through milestones checked off like items on a never-ending to-do list.

With unwavering determination, I forged ahead. Amid mounting physical exhaustion and the emotional whirlwind of impending motherhood, I focused my energy and delivered. I completed and published both the research paper and the review article before my baby arrived—an achievement that felt like crossing a finish line I had set for myself. And when it was done, I felt a profound sense of accomplishment—not just for what I had produced, but for having honored the commitment I made to myself, even as life was preparing to change in the most beautiful and unpredictable ways.

On a cold January night, a mother was born alongside her daughter. My husband and I had walked this journey together, eagerly awaiting the arrival of our baby girl. When she finally came into our world, we named her Aadrika, a Sanskrit word that translates to "Celestial" in English—a name befitting the source of our renewed strength and love.

Parenthood was a beautiful and transformative experience, yet it was also uncharted territory, filled with sleepless nights, countless diaper changes, and moments of exhaustion. In those first three months after Aadrika was born, time felt like it had melted into one long, endless day.

I remember one night—or maybe it was morning, I couldn't keep track anymore—when she had been crying for hours. I had tried everything: feeding, changing, rocking her, walking laps around the living room with her cradled in my arms. My back ached, my eyes were heavy, and my voice was hoarse from singing lullabies in a loop.

Around 4:30 a.m., I sat on the edge of the bed, holding her close, both of us teetering between exhaustion and surrender. I looked out the window. The world outside was quiet, sleeping, while I sat inside, my shirt stained with milk and tears silently rolling down my cheeks. It wasn't sadness exactly; it was something deeper. A reckoning. The woman I had been—precise, efficient, always in control—no longer existed in the same way.

I remember whispering to Aadrika in the dim light, "I don't know what I'm doing, but I promise I'll figure it out for you." It wasn't a moment of triumph; it was a moment of vulnerability, of truth. A breaking and a rebuilding.

I finally understood what motherhood is all about. It's far more complicated than I thought; it's the most beautiful feeling, but also the most challenging task to do and be committed to. The sleepless nights, the exhaustion, the identity shifts—these are real problems. Your hormones are acting up, it feels like everything is against you, and yet you still have to survive.

I was not prepared. My mom never told me all these things because, I think, her generation never discussed them. The girls of my generation grew up quickly and didn't have the opportunity to learn about the trials of motherhood. But as an educated, self-valued person with a working, logical mind, when I became a new mother, I asked myself, Where do I start? How do I crack this code?

It was so difficult. I was wearing the hat of a logical, professional, self-executing person, breaking down the situation into pieces, block by block, but nothing was working. Aadrika often wouldn't fall asleep until 5:00 a.m., and I found myself thinking, I've never passed time in this manner before. It may sound detached, even cold, but that was my honest reality. I've always placed immense value on time—measured it in outcomes, productivity, and progress. So, those long, sleepless nights spent cradling my child and singing lullabies into the quiet darkness felt disorienting at first. As a professional accustomed to structure and purpose, I struggled to reconcile this new rhythm where presence—not performance—was the only requirement.

Over time, though, something shifts. The metrics by which you once measured your worth begin to evolve. Slowly, you surrender to the messiness, the unpredictability, the quiet beauty of this new life. You don't just adapt; you are transformed. And in that transformation, you discover that not all value is quantifiable. Sometimes, you encounter the most meaningful moments in the spaces where nothing seems to be happening, yet everything is changing.

Was I prepared for this drastic life change? I was prepared to be a mom, but as for what it entailed, what it cost, and what it really and truly asked of me, I wasn't. I felt like I had been hit by a train. As the days turned into weeks, I found myself eventually transformed. My priorities shifted, and my daughter became the center of my universe.

After three precious months with Aadrika, I made the difficult decision to return to work. I didn't feel like I had to earn that time off—no one was forcing me to keep going, either at work or at home. But I never really felt like my job was a job. I felt that I had two babies. I was fully committed to my first baby, my career, and my second baby, my daughter. I had to take care of my career first so that I could happily enjoy my baby. I'd made a commitment. I didn't want my research projects to suffer, and I wanted to make sure that Aadrika was taken care of.

Like many working parents in the U.S., my husband and I navigated the complexities of balancing our careers and caring for our child. We shared responsibilities, took turns caring for her when she was sick, and made every effort to be present for her milestones. Thankfully, my husband has been nothing short of a rock—steady, unwavering, and endlessly supportive. With his help, I was able to make things work for me and everyone around me.

I valued my professional role as deeply as I cherished being a mother. Also, I feared losing out on opportunities if I took a longer maternity leave. Why are there still so few women in CEO or leadership roles? Too often, it's because they're forced to choose between their careers and their children. It's not a matter of lacking ambition or ability, but the burden of an unfair choice. In a world that rarely makes space for both, women are pulled in opposite directions, expected to give wholly to one while silently surrendering the other. This is where many women find themselves at a disadvantage in the workplace, not due to a lack of talent or dedication, but because the playing field is far from even. It's not about competition with men—I hold deep respect for them—but rather about navigating an environment that hasn't yet fully adapted to support the unique challenges women often face.

Women often have to choose between caring for their child and their work. And when you go back to work, you don't even know what you have missed. You don't even know where to start, where to pick up the pieces. You return to work, perhaps two steps behind in your profession, because of this beautiful thing that happened in your life. You are paying a cost. That's not what a man experiences.

These are real issues. We lose opportunities. We lose our confidence. We lose our hold, our relevance, and our power when we return to work after an extended maternity leave, and I didn't want that to happen. Remember, I want to "have it all," and I'm ready to pay the cost. So, are you ready to pay the cost? A significant cost is involved for a successful and ambitious woman in this world. That is the reality and truth.

I had to compartmentalize. I had to say, "Okay, I'm going to use resources and accept help and be more strategic about this. I'm not going to give up my work and be flooded with emotions to the point where I can't function. I'm going to take care of my child with the help of others, and I'm going to excel in my career."

In the U.S., fortunately, I was able to afford those resources. I put my baby in a reliable daycare, so she received the care she needed while I took care of my work and the world I had built. We visited her at daycare and, of course, spent time with her in the evenings. I took everything into my own hands and led my research team as if nothing had changed in my life, even though everything had changed. I made the transition look seamless. You must learn to navigate those challenges if you wish to thrive in a world still shaped primarily by masculine norms and expectations.

Motherhood was still far more demanding than I had anticipated. Despite my best efforts, I felt overwhelmed, juggling work, childcare, and the constant fatigue that accompanied both. I watched my daughter grow, witnessing her first steps and her first words, yet exhaustion clouded my joy.

My daily routine was relentless: rushing to daycare, working long hours, picking her up, feeding her, bathing her, and then enduring sleepless nights. It was during these months of exhaustion and solitude that I deeply longed for my mother.

I had always seen myself as a fearless, resilient, and nearly invincible woman. But behind closed doors, I realized that even the strongest women can feel vulnerable. Motherhood unveiled a truth I had never fully grasped before: When you are at your weakest, the only person who truly understands you is your mother.

Acknowledging my limits, I accepted that I needed help. My husband supported me as much as he could, but the reality of societal expectations weighed heavily on me. Despite our household's egalitarian approach to chores, the responsibility of childcare felt disproportionately mine, not because it was imposed upon me, but because my instincts, meticulous nature, and unwavering sense of duty wouldn't allow me to trust anyone else with it.

I guess that's what every new mother goes through. This perfectionism, though, came at a cost. I was exhausted, emotionally drained, and neglecting my own well-being. Many women go through this phase, especially first-time mothers living far from family support. However, I refused to pity myself. I reminded myself that I was capable, strong, and determined to push through. I motivated myself daily, refusing to lose my sense of self.

As an ambitious, self-driven mother, I had responsibilities beyond childcare alone—my career, my aspirations, and my identity. Still, motherhood remained the most challenging role I had ever taken on.

Through this journey, I learned patience and resilience, and I developed a newfound appreciation for the sacrifices mothers make. My goal now is to lead by example, raising my daughter with the strength and wisdom I've gained while honoring the lessons my mother taught me.

Most importantly, I came to understand that mothers are not divine figures of endless sacrifice. They are human beings with dreams, desires, and emotions. They should be valued as individuals. Too often, we take them for granted, expecting them to be unwavering pillars of support without acknowledging their own needs. It is time to shift our perspective.

Women of flesh and blood deserve care, recognition, and love beyond their roles as caregivers. I believe it is our duty, as members of the sandwich generation—those of us with living parents and children of our own—to implement this paradigm shift. As a daughter, I saw motherhood through a different lens. But when I became a mother, I began to see things in a different light. I struggle every day to change the perception of motherhood, and I may never have it all figured out. I am doing my best to balance it all.

There are moments when I break down, collapse, and cry, and I don't fear showing my tears to my daughter or husband. I let them know that I need help. I let them know that I'm more than a caregiver and a support system for them. I have my own needs. I am an individual with dreams and aspirations, and I need self-care, as well as care from them. I think that's what was missing in my life growing up: seeing a mother be cared for.

My mom always put her children and her husband first. It was as if she was a machine, only good for providing solutions, support, and resources for our immediate and extended family. Sadly, that is what we have reduced our women to, with no sense of value, no sense of time, no sense of their needs. Me, my sisters, my father, my aunts, uncles, and cousins—they all took priority. She did not prioritize herself. And though it pains me to admit it, no one in our family—including myself—ever stopped to ask her, "What do you need? Do you need love, support, or simply a moment to breathe?" We were so focused on what she gave, we never paused to see what she might need in return.

My mother never asked for love in return, never pleaded to be seen as a person with dreams and needs of her own. She never said, "Think of me, care for me, understand me." The truth is, she had quietly let go of those expectations long ago, sacrificing her own desires to give everything to those she loved.

Now that I'm a mother, I understand how we placed my mom on a pedestal—out of deep respect, yes, but also perhaps as a way to compensate for all the years she gave without ever asking for anything in return. Yet I've come to realize that most mothers, including myself, don't long to be idolized. We don't want to be worshipped; we want to be seen, heard, and held as human beings, not revered as untouchable saints.

I want my family to understand me as a human being. I have my own aspirations, desires, and life, so I need the same care and love that I'm giving to them. I want to make sure that my daughter understands this. Some days, it's hard, and some days, it's not. Some days, she understands, and some days, she doesn't. But I never stop leading by example and showing her that my needs are just as important as anyone else's.

I don't want my daughter to one day find herself standing at the crossroads of identity and motherhood, asking, What happened to me? Why did I choose to be a mother? I want her to walk into that chapter of her life—if she chooses it—not burdened by sacrifice, but enriched by the memory of being nurtured by a woman who embraced both love and ambition with grace.

These days, every time I call my mother, I find myself saying, "Thank you, Mom." Thank you for your quiet resilience in the face of storms I was too young to understand. Thank you for teaching me strength not through grand speeches, but through your everyday choices. Thank you for being my anchor, my guide, and your unwavering presence as I was shaping the earliest contours of my life. Thank you for showing me that motherhood is not the erasure of self, but the reimagining of it.

Through those simple words—spoken now with the depth of a fellow mother—I am finally beginning to understand the magnitude of what it means to give, to love, and to grow beside your child.

But somehow, the words still feel inadequate. My mother no longer needs a "thank you"—it's too late for that. She should have told us what she needed, but she never did. And now, all we're left with is the silence where her needs once lived, unspoken and unmet. So, I am doing a course correction. I am teaching my daughter every day when I say, "I need my time. I am taking some time for myself to relax." Or,

"You have to do your own work because Mommy needs to get her work done." Or, "I have a responsibility towards my professional career; it is important to me." I want her to hear these things every day, to see me prioritizing myself, so that when she's my age, she won't be thanking me for sacrificing myself. When she is my age, I want her to be able to speak up for herself, just as I am doing.

We mothers must use our voices to be heard by our partners, family members, and society. My mother did not use her voice to stand up for herself, but she did use her voice to stand up for my sisters and me, and I am carrying that into raising my own daughter. But I'm also applying the things that I have learned. It's a very hard journey. That's why I say that even though I have done so much in my life—earned promotions, won awards, and achieved degrees—motherhood has been the toughest of them all. I want to be respected, valued, and seen, not as a service provider, but as a human being with dignity, depth, and dreams of my own. As working, ambitious moms, we must make the next generation understand that they need to respect us and our time just as we respect them for what they do. Don't take us for granted. Value the sacrifices we are making.

One day, my daughter said to me, "You are available more than Daddy because you have more time." I told her immediately, "I have just as much work to do as your dad, and I am investing time to make you my priority. If I have to do my work at night while you are sleeping, I will, so that I can spend time with you. It's not that I'm available because I don't have anything to do. Please don't forget that."

Conversations like these between mothers and daughters are what will bring a shift in the mindset from one generation to the next.

As I mentioned earlier, there is an overwhelming pressure when you want to "have it all." Some days are very, very rough. It feels like your spirit is broken. Some days, you buckle up and force yourself to rise again above the horizon, above the dirt, and get going. To do that, you need a lot of resilience, support, and mental strength—more than men possess. And then there is the fatigue, guilt, and fear of losing out at work. All these dynamics are playing in your mind.

It is an incredibly challenging path for a young mother, a new mother, or any mother who finds herself balancing countless responsibilities, unwilling to let a single ball fall. Choosing motherhood is not a fault; it is a profound and courageous decision. And yet, too often, it feels as though that choice is met not with grace, but with invisible penalties—almost as if bringing a new life into the world is a burden to be borne alone.

There are days of deep loneliness, and others where the warmth of support offers a brief reprieve. But through it all, you persist. You carry on, whether by biting the bullet, holding your breath, or simply placing one foot in front of the other. Because you must. And if you can endure those moments—however heavy they feel—you will survive. And not just survive, but perhaps even emerge stronger.

In our marriage, equality isn't a principle we preach—it's a rhythm we live by. Shrikant and I share the responsibilities of daily life with quiet understanding and mutual respect. He is never hesitant to roll up his sleeves to wash the dishes, prepare a meal, or do the laundry. And I, in turn, approach both domestic duties and professional ambitions with equal commitment.

There is no scoreboard in our home, no tallying of who did what. Instead, there's a deep sense of partnership—a belief that building a life together means supporting each other fully, whether it's in the personal or professional space. Our marriage is rooted in balance, where neither role is fixed and every contribution is valued. In this shared space, love is expressed not just in words, but in actions that say: "We're in this together."

I consider myself fortunate, but with that gratitude comes a deep desire for perfection. I carry a vision in my heart: the life I want for my child, the impact I hope to make through my work, the harmony I seek in my personal life, and the warmth I wish to cultivate at home. This is the quiet paradox of being an ambitious mother—a journey that is both profoundly fulfilling and immensely demanding. Balancing it all is not simply about time management; it's about emotional endurance, clarity of purpose, and constant recalibration. It is a responsibility that reshapes you, and one that you should only embrace when you're truly ready, for it is one of the most intricate, beautiful, and challenging relationships life will ever ask you to navigate.

When I watch my daughter shine on stage, echoing the very steps I once took as a child, I see a reflection of myself—a little mirror of who I was and who I continue to be. In those moments, when others come up to me and say, "She's so much like you," "You're raising her with such beautiful values," or "She's incredibly talented and full of life," my heart overflows with quiet pride.

These words aren't just compliments; they are affirmations of the love, thought, and intention I pour into raising her. Each day, I ask myself the same question: Am I doing this right? And each day, in her grace, her kindness, and her spark, I find my answer. I may not have all the answers, but I know I am doing something right.

No matter what unfolds in my life, one promise remains unwavering: to honor and carry forward the legacy of my family. This silent yet powerful commitment fuels my pursuit of excellence in my career and my personal life, and especially in motherhood.

My message for young girls and first-time mothers: Motherhood is a transformative journey that tests resilience, redefines identity, and challenges the myth of having it all. Balancing ambition and family comes with sacrifices, but true strength lies in acknowledging our limits and seeking support. Mothers are not meant to be silent warriors of sacrifice. They are people with dreams, aspirations, and the right to self-care. Let's uplift, support, and celebrate women, not just as caregivers but as whole, empowered beings.

CHAPTER 7

My MBA Journey: Balancing Motherhood, Ambition, and Growth

Before I became a mother, my focus was razor-sharp, and my commitment to my career felt absolute—steady, unquestioned, and deeply fulfilling. But with motherhood came a quiet, complex paradox: a gentle yet unrelenting current of guilt that began to flow beneath even my proudest achievements. Questions I had never asked myself before began to echo in the stillness between tasks and meetings: Am I doing enough for my daughter? Am I present in the ways that matter? Will she be okay without me while I chase these ambitions?

These questions didn't stem from doubt in my abilities, but from the depth of my love and the impossible desire to give wholly to both worlds. It is in this delicate tension that the true journey of working motherhood unfolds, not as a failure of balance, but as a testament to the strength it takes to pursue both purpose and presence.

These questions echoed not from a place of doubt in my love, but from unfamiliarity. I had never seen my own mother navigate the duality of a career and motherhood. Her devotion was singular, wholly focused on raising us. And so, as I chart a path she never walked, I find myself forging "a new model of motherhood"—one filled with questions, compromises, and constant recalibrations. Yet, in this delicate balancing act, I am discovering not weakness, but strength.

My mother's sacrifices laid the foundation for my journey, and I sometimes question if I'm doing justice to all the struggles she endured, to the path she carved for me. But then I remind myself that progress demands change. If everything remains the same, then what was the purpose of all those sacrifices? My mother did not have the opportunity or the support to build a thriving career, but I do. Walking away from a fulfilling profession after years of effort and ambition would be a disservice not only to myself but also to the legacy I carry and all the people who believe in me.

My soul wrestled with this conflict, but I stood firm, trusting that my daughter would thrive even as I stepped away to build something greater. And she did. The first year of motherhood was a whirlwind, but as my daughter's routine settled, so did my thoughts. I knew I needed to take a bold step, not just for my career but for the larger impact I aspire to make. Inspired by the remarkable trajectory of my mentor at the Cancer Center, I decided to elevate my journey.

It was a beautiful March day, with spring's promise in the air, when I sat down with my husband to have an important discussion. Until that moment, he had no idea what had been stirring in my mind. With a one-year-old at home, most wouldn't consider making a major career move, but I had already begun researching MBA programs and weighing the options. Whether to relocate or stay close, scholarships, internships, and the financial and logistical challenges—all these factors swirled in my mind. My husband sat in stunned silence, listening as I spoke, absorbing the magnitude of what I was proposing.

He took some time to think, and the very next day, he was ready to support my dreams. He didn't dismiss them. Instead, he said, "We have to figure this out." He is an incredible human being, not only for his love and support but for the depth of thought he brings to every decision.

The road ahead was anything but simple. With my chosen program demanding a two-hour daily commute, we had to consider hiring a nanny, restructuring our daily routines, and even the possibility of my husband changing jobs. The financial implications loomed large, making a scholarship essential.

Every factor demanded careful deliberation, and every decision required courage and faith. Then, everything started to fall into place. I secured a seventy percent scholarship in the form of multiple awards. In an act of profound support, my husband made a career shift, choosing a job closer to home so he could take on more parental responsibilities while I pursued my education. In return, I made sure my husband's career was in no way reduced or compromised in his continued ascent in the value chain.

My MBA was never just about a degree. It was a declaration of resilience, a testament to the power of partnership, and a radical act of self-belief. Through this journey, I learned that success isn't about choosing between ambition and family. It is about building a life where both can thrive. And as I pave this path, I hope to create a world where more women feel empowered to chase their dreams without carrying the impossible weight of guilt. A world where choosing oneself is not an act of defiance but a celebration of possibility, where ambition and motherhood are not opposing forces but intertwined strengths.

This journey was never mine alone; it was ours—my daughter's and my husband's, woven together in a shared vision of what is possible. As I stand here today, I know without a doubt that I made the right choice. It took us a year to meticulously arrange every moving piece before I could begin business school. Choosing the right nanny was an exhaustive process, one we approached with the utmost precision. Yet, even with everything in place, stepping into this new chapter was daunting.

The first six months were particularly grueling. Coming from a rigorous biology background, I suddenly found myself grappling with subjects like accounting and finance that felt entirely foreign. I sat in the front row, asked innumerable questions, and poured myself into every lecture, project, and discussion. My days were a relentless cycle of classes, group studies, and projects, stretching late into the night. I would return home around 10:30 or 11:00 p.m., exhausted yet wired. I was in go mode—driven, focused, and determined. My efforts were visible to everyone around me.

I barely saw my daughter, although she was always in my thoughts. I was deeply grateful for our nanny, who helped keep our home afloat, but the guilt of being an absent mother weighed heavily on me. The only times I could momentarily silence the ache of missing her were during lectures or when I was engrossed in a project presentation. My only moments of respite were the late-night meals shared with my husband, my steadfast partner and sounding board. He never ate until I came home, waiting to sit beside me, offering quiet encouragement and unwavering support.

I felt an unrelenting need to push myself even harder. After all, I was competing with students who had no distractions or responsibilities beyond their studies.

Then, one day, my daughter fell ill at daycare. She was only two and a half years old—still so small, still needing me for everything. When I came home, I saw that her tiny body was burning with fever. Her cheeks were flushed, and she clung to me, whimpering, her normally curious eyes dulled by exhaustion.

I had an important exam the next morning, one that I had prepared for over weeks. But in that moment, all that planning dissolved into irrelevance. There was only one decision to make. I cradled my daughter in my arms. I rocked her gently and sponged her forehead again and again as she drifted in and out of restless sleep. I could feel her rapid breathing against my chest, and every tiny stir or cry pulled at me with the weight of helplessness.

Inside, I felt like I was unraveling.

I sat by her side, textbooks spread open beside me, highlighter in one hand and thermometer in the other. I tried to read—tried to keep going—but every few minutes, I'd have to stop. Her cough. Her cry. Her need. The maternal instinct in me was louder than any ambition.

At one point in the early hours, around 3 a.m., I remember looking in the mirror while washing her fevered cloth. I looked exhausted—eyes swollen, hair a mess, worry etched into every feature. I felt like I was failing both worlds. Not present enough for my child, not focused enough for my exam.

And yet, somewhere in that blur of anxiety and exhaustion, a quiet strength stirred. Not the loud, confident kind, but the tired, determined kind that keeps you going when you're completely depleted. I reminded myself that this was a phase. That being here, holding her through this night, was just as important as any exam.

That night taught me something I carry with me still: Strength doesn't always look like having it all together. Sometimes, it's sitting on the floor at 2 a.m. with a sick child in your lap and a half-read textbook beside you, whispering to yourself, "You're doing the best you can." And sometimes, that's more than enough.

At dawn, I walked into my exam hall, drained but determined. I had already done the work hours earlier. Preparation had become my safety net, allowing me to rise above the inevitable hurdles. I performed well, but this was just one instance in an ongoing balancing act, a tightrope I walked daily, knowing that my scholarship, my future, and the foundation of my family all depended on my ability to persist.

Through it all, I became acutely aware of my husband's sacrifices. He shouldered so much to keep our family steady, never wavering in his belief in me. I was fortunate to have him, along with a network of mentors and friends who uplifted me. However, I couldn't ignore the stark reality faced by many women around me. I often saw young women supported by their parents, but rarely by their spouses or broader communities. This is why women struggle to accelerate their careers at the same pace as men. I was privileged. I never had to diverge from the trajectory of my male peers because I had a solid, unwavering support system, but this is not the reality for most women.

I want to advocate for sustainable support systems that empower women to thrive, not just survive. I've had countless conversations with my American women colleagues, many of whom have shared how they juggle education, careers, and households, often without a strong support network. The situation is no different in India, where women are expected to be full-time mothers and wives while simultaneously excelling in their careers. The burden is immense. The expectation is relentless. It is a system set up for exhaustion, for failure. It shouldn't be this way. Women deserve support, not sacrifice. This is not a privilege; it is a necessity. We must reshape the system to make success sustainable for all.

As I look back, I am profoundly grateful for my husband's unwavering support. Without him, the intricate balance of my life—part-time work, full-time MBA classes, and endless hours of studying—would have remained a distant dream. Unlike so many women, I was not burdened with unrealistic expectations while navigating these demanding roles. That, in itself, was a privilege.

I still remember a conversation with a male colleague who was in a situation quite similar to mine. He shared his challenges and then smiled, almost with relief, and said, "I am only doing my MBA. My wife is raising our two kids, and honestly, I don't know much about what happens at home." His words echoed long after they were spoken, stirring a profound and unsettling awareness within me. The impact was sudden and jarring—like a sharp slap across the face—forcing me to confront truths I had been avoiding and to see myself through a clearer, harsher lens.

Men get to "have it all" without even thinking twice about what's happening in their home because their wives are taking care of it all. Women get to "have it all" and die trying because we are expected to be in charge of everything at home alongside a career, if that's our choice. I couldn't help but wonder if that colleague's wife also had a job in addition to managing their household and kids. The double standard is maddening. Yes, my situation was better than that of many working women, but the irony was undeniable.

Despite my relentless, fifteen-hour days, filled with travel, coursework, and professional commitments, I still knew every detail of my household. I knew what my nanny was preparing for each meal and what my daughter was doing every moment of the day. The silent, ingrained expectation of managing both spheres—home and career—never fully disappeared. So, I asked myself, Will the narrative be different for my daughter?

I want a world where she feels truly empowered to chase her ambitions, unencumbered by the weight of societal expectations that dictate how she should balance her career and motherhood. A world where she does not have to choose between being a nurturing mother and a driven professional, but where both identities can coexist seamlessly and without guilt. A world where ambition is not just questioned, where support is not seen as a luxury but as a given. For her and every daughter, we must reshape this reality, not just in whispers of hope but through tangible change.

Earning my MBA was far more than the pursuit of another credential; it was a defining chapter of resilience, determination, and the quiet defiance of societal expectations. It marked a bold pivot from my deep-rooted, research-intensive background in biochemistry and oncology to the dynamic, fast-paced world of business within medicine. The transition was anything but easy. It demanded that I step outside the familiar language of science and immerse myself in the complexities of strategy, leadership, and market dynamics. It was daunting. There were expectations, spoken and unspoken, about where I belonged and what paths were acceptable. But I knew that to truly make an impact in healthcare, I had to bridge the gap between science and strategy. Pursuing my MBA was a conscious decision to step out of my comfort zone. It meant late nights, countless sacrifices, and moments of self-doubt. But it also meant proving to myself and others that I could navigate both worlds.

During my MBA, I was honored to receive the Joel E. Scholarship Award, the Harmon Pearl Scholarship Award, and the Nicholas and Nancy J. Balaria MB Fellowship in recognition of my academic excellence and merit. I was proud of these awards because I demonstrated that a woman in science could just as seamlessly step into leadership, strategy, and business decision-making.

One of the most valuable lessons from my MBA experience was the power of partnership. Balancing work, studies, and family life required unwavering support. I had to learn that asking for help wasn't a weakness; it was a strategy for success. My husband, my mentors, and my peers played pivotal roles in lifting me when I needed it most. Perseverance became my constant companion. There were moments when exhaustion took over, but I learned that true strength lies in pushing forward, even when the road is unclear. My MBA also reinforced my sense of self-worth, that I deserved a seat at the table, that my voice mattered, and that my ambitions were valid. Most importantly, this journey changed my definition of success.

It's no longer about titles or external validation. Success, to me, is about having the freedom and choice to shape my path, make meaningful contributions, and uplift others along the way. For more women to pursue their ambitions without carrying an impossible burden, systemic and cultural changes are needed. We need workplace structures that truly support working mothers. We need to redefine what success means and how to achieve balance. Also, we need stronger networks of support. We need women to uplift each other, share their experiences, and create spaces where ambition and motherhood are not seen as opposing forces. Everything I have done so far—the degrees, the articles and papers, the research projects—has led me to this moment. The realization that I can be a force for change in helping women to see themselves as capable, whole, and deserving. This is my life's goal, my next mission.

My message for women and girls who are still debating whether to take their next career move: Balancing ambition and personal growth is a test of resilience, sacrifice, and unwavering determination. Women are often allowed to dream, but then face guilt, societal expectations, and systemic challenges when attempting to carry out those dreams. True progress occurs when women are not only encouraged to pursue their goals but also provided with the necessary support to achieve their full potential. Let's create a world where women don't have to choose between family and career but are empowered to succeed at both.

CHAPTER 8

Beyond the Pandemic: Resolving to Build Meaningful Connections

Just as I was completing my MBA, the unimaginable struck: the COVID-19 pandemic. We had so many dreams and plans as a family, all waiting to be fulfilled after two long years of sacrifice. We were planning a trip to Europe to celebrate my success in my MBA journey and the completion of another milestone. Then the world came crashing down, and I couldn't wrap my head around any of it. This was not something I had ever experienced, or even anticipated, and I didn't know what to do. There was widespread fear, isolation, and global panic, and we were feeling it deeply, along with everyone else.

Instead of celebrating, we found ourselves grappling with fear and uncertainty, prioritizing ways to simply survive. The joy of my graduation—marked by awards, an internship, and a prestigious job at a top consulting organization—was overshadowed by the pressing need to protect our lives. I felt sad and disappointed. We celebrated as a family, which I am grateful for, but I didn't get to experience the festivities to their fullest since we were on lockdown.

As we were adjusting to this new reality, an even greater tragedy struck. I lost my father, and my mother was left alone and heartbroken in India. International travel was restricted, leaving her to bear the weight of this profound loss on her own. But even in the face of grief, she stood tall, showing resilience and strength beyond measure. Once again, she became my beacon, offering silent lessons through her actions.

Before we could process our grief, another devastating blow followed: we lost my mother-in-law. The pain of these back-to-back losses left us vulnerable, deeply saddened, and struggling to find meaning. It felt as though the very foundation of our lives had crumbled. Shrikant and I had to juggle our demanding jobs while homeschooling our daughter, all while carrying the weight of immense sorrow.

Life seemed to be unraveling, yet my mother's strength remained a guiding force. While I was locked indoors, deprived of human contact, caught in an endless cycle of work, household chores, and caregiving, life began to feel like an unending imprisonment. I found myself changed in ways I hadn't anticipated. My worldly accomplishments, once a source of pride, suddenly seemed hollow. The ambitions that had always fueled me were devoid of meaning.

I often find myself caught in a relentless rhythm—always running, always reaching, chasing after the next goal without allowing space to simply pause and breathe. I've asked myself, time and again, Why this constant urgency? Why this unyielding desire to prove myself, to be seen, to be validated?

Over time, I've come to realize that this impulse is not arbitrary. It's the echo of a silent vow I made long ago—a deeply embedded thread of childhood conditioning. It is the legacy of a father I adored and admired, a man whose brilliance and drive shaped not only his path but cast long, reverent shadows on mine. Somewhere along the way, I internalized an unspoken promise: to carry forward his flame, to honor his name, to prove worthy of the love and sacrifices that shaped me.

In doing so, I began to tether my worth to accomplishments. Every accolade became a stepping stone, every milestone a symbol that I was enough. I needed to win people over—not out of vanity, but out of a deeply ingrained need to be recognized, to be worthy, to belong. I became fluent in the languages of achievement and ambition.

Even now, my mind remains wired to that tempo—a familiar, almost comforting rhythm of striving. There are moments when I see through it, when the pursuit feels hollow, and I wonder what it would be like to "just be." And yet, this is the cadence of my life. I am, at my core, a dreamer and a doer, always reaching, always building, always moving toward the next horizon. It is my gift and my burden, my inheritance and my truth.

The pandemic, in its quiet and chaos, became an unexpected mirror, forcing me into stillness, into uncomfortable yet necessary introspection. For as long as I could remember, I had defined happiness by a narrow lens: achievements, accolades, the applause of others. Success was my compass, and external validation was the fuel that kept me moving. But somewhere along the way, I had forgotten to ask myself the simplest, most essential question: Am I truly happy?

That realization struck me with the force of lightning—sudden, jarring, and impossible to ignore. I saw myself for what I had become: someone who relentlessly chased milestones, checking off boxes, reaching goal after goal without ever savoring the journey. I was living in fast-forward, mistaking motion for meaning.

In the silence of isolation, my mind grew louder. Whispered doubts became urgent questions: What truly differentiates me from a machine? Have I reduced myself to a life of metrics, devoid of presence and pause? When, if ever, will I slow down enough to feel the life I'm living?

The answers didn't come easily, but what did emerge was a shift—a profound unraveling and reweaving of my perspective. I began to see the world not as a series of benchmarks to conquer, but as a canvas to experience. I no longer defined my place in it by how much I could accomplish, but by how deeply I could feel, connect, and be.

The pandemic changed many things, but perhaps its most lasting gift was this: the permission to step back, to question the life I had built, and to begin, gently, to live more deliberately.

For the first time, I confronted a quiet truth that had long lived in the shadows of my ambition—one I had skillfully ignored for years. I had moved through life with purpose, yes, but also with a kind of emotional detachment. I had never allowed myself the simple joy of sitting alone on a park bench, soaking in the rustle of leaves, the rhythm of birdsong, the dance of sunlight on water. I had been present in body, but absent in soul.

I realized, too, that I had seldom nurtured the bonds that make life rich with warmth and resonance. Where was my tribe? Why had I never built a circle of close, lifelong female friendships—a "girl's gang" that could hold me in laughter and in sorrow? Somewhere along the way, I had mistaken independence for isolation, and productivity for fulfillment.

The question loomed, stark and honest: Would my life amount to nothing more than a curated list of accomplishments? Or was there still time to craft something deeper, fuller, and more human?

Loss, when it came, was intimate and shattering. It stripped away the noise and the armor, revealing the fragile truths we often outrun. It forced me to pause, to reflect on the impermanence of all things. Death, I came to understand, is life's only certainty. The way we choose to live, the love we give and receive, the memories we leave behind—those are ours to shape.

And so, I began to reimagine my existence, not as a race to be won, but as a life to be felt. A life marked not just by success, but by connection. By presence. By meaning.

I began to worry that, in my relentless pursuit of excellence, I was slowly drifting away from the very essence of being "human"—becoming detached from the richness of emotion, from the quiet, tender moments that give life its meaning. If I were to survive this terrible time and see a world beyond COVID-19, I knew I had to make a change. That's when I shifted my priorities and ambitions. I resolved to invest in relationships and build connections that were not just transactional but deeply human. I vowed to strengthen bonds with my family, forge genuine friendships, and cultivate trusted partnerships, both personally and professionally.

⁂

After years of sprinting toward goals—stacking degrees, meeting deadlines, and embracing new roles with enthusiasm—I found myself in an unfamiliar emotional space: stillness. Due to the dramatic pause of the pandemic, I felt a slow, creeping realization that somewhere along the way, in my fierce commitment to building a fulfilling life, I had allowed something quietly essential to erode: connection.

Connection, not just in the perfunctory sense of greetings or scheduled phone calls, but the kind that roots you, nourishes you, and makes the success worth something. So, I made a quiet vow, an inward recalibration. I would no longer let meaningful relationships become unintended casualties of ambition. I would not just balance but prioritize the bonds with my family, the friendships I had once held dear, and the working relationships that had the potential to be more than transactional.

It began, not with grand reunions or sweeping apologies, but with small, mindful choices.

With friends, I began the long-overdue act of reaching out. It was humbling to trace my roots and find them scattered across time zones and life stages, raising families, writing books, and leading teams. To my surprise, many had been looking for me. Their messages were warm, tinged with curiosity and something else—an enduring affection. They hadn't forgotten me.

There was a moment I remember distinctly: a voice message from an old school friend saying, "We wondered where you vanished to. You were always the dreamer among us; we knew you'd be doing something amazing. We just missed you." I sat with that message for a long time. The tenderness in it, the quiet forgiveness. I hadn't even known I needed it.

When we finally spoke—laughing over long-forgotten teachers, old mischiefs, and bittersweet stories—it was like a part of myself I had locked away had found its way back. We were different, of course, but the fabric of our connection remained intact. It wasn't nostalgia; it was recognition. A reclaiming of something essential.

With my mother, the shift was less visible but more profound. I began calling her each evening, not to check in as the "dutiful" daughter, but to truly listen to her voice. Our conversations meandered about her neighbor or a dream she had the night before. These small, inconsequential things became the architecture of our intimacy.

Over time, she began telling me stories I had only heard in fragments before—how she learned to manage her home as a young bride, how my father got his first job. These were more than just anecdotes. They were pieces of a legacy I had once overlooked and now gathered with quiet reverence.

One evening, after she walked me through her signature fish curry recipe over the phone and waited patiently as I struggled to follow her "add by instinct" instructions, she said, "You sound calmer these days. You don't rush through our calls anymore. I like that." It was simple, yet so powerful. Her words lingered longer with me than I expected.

They were an affirmation, not just of her love, but of a version of me I was learning to rediscover.

At work, I shifted in smaller, quieter ways. I stopped showing up only as the problem-solver or strategist and began leading with empathy. I remembered that my colleagues, like me, carried invisible burdens. When one teammate confided her struggle adjusting to a new role, I didn't just offer advice—I sat with her after hours, helping her build a plan she could own. When another lost a loved one, I sent her a handwritten note. No one asked me to do it, and I certainly didn't have the perfect words to say, but I wanted her to feel that I was there for her.

These weren't acts of heroism. They were invitations to trust, to connect, to be human. And over time, the culture around me responded. People began to open up more. There was more laughter in meetings, more patience during setbacks, more generosity in praise. The air shifted.

And then, slowly, something remarkable began to happen: the energy I had been putting into the world—the kindness, the attention, the care—began to return. Not always directly, not always immediately, but unmistakably. A colleague offered to take over a presentation when I had to leave work early to attend to my daughter. A friend from my past mailed me a book she thought I'd love, with a note that simply read: "This made me think of you."

The reciprocation was never the goal, but it became a gift of grace.

The promise I had made—to be present, to reach out, to show up—transformed the shape of my days. It taught me that relationships don't ask for perfection, just presence. Showing up doesn't require grand gestures; it just requires quiet consistency. That love, whether in friendship, family, or work, isn't built in one moment, but in the patient stitching together of many small ones. And perhaps most humbling of all, it reminded me that in being there for others, I found my own way back to myself.

Life is not just about the milestones we reach, but also about the moments we share, the lives we touch, and the warmth we leave behind. This experience reshaped me, offering a perspective I never had before. Now, I teach my daughter not only to work hard and chase her dreams but also to nurture relationships that add meaning and joy to her life. Success is always going to be there, but you need those trusted relationships, those cheerleaders, those people whom you love and connect with, to be there, to celebrate with you, to give you a sense of togetherness. In my pursuit of success and excellence, I often ignored the significance of human connection. The pandemic taught me to nurture my relationships. Sometimes, the darkest moments bring forth the most profound lessons, ones that success alone could never teach.

Consider this: There is undeniable merit in striving for financial and material independence. It is both empowering and practical to seek stability, to build a life of security and self-sufficiency. There is honor in ambition, in the pursuit of goals that reflect discipline, resilience, and purpose. To be able to stand on your own, to provide for yourself and those you love, is a testament to strength, and it deserves recognition.

But beyond this tangible success lies another form of wealth—one far less visible, yet infinitely more profound. It is the wealth of the heart:

love freely given and received, the quiet strength of emotional support, the comfort of being truly seen and understood. It resides in deep connections, in shared laughter, in the kind of companionship that silences loneliness and magnifies joy.

While material abundance can cushion life's hardships and offer convenience, it is this second kind of wealth that breathes life into our days. It is what nourishes the soul in moments of doubt, celebrates with us in times of triumph, and holds us steady when everything else begins to shift.

True fulfillment is not found in what we own, but in who we become and how we love. It's in the richness of our relationships, the warmth of belonging, and the legacy of kindness we leave behind. And so, while we strive for worldly success, let us also invest in the currency of connection—for it is this wealth that endures, that deepens with time, and that ultimately gives life its most meaningful measure.

The message for my readers: The COVID-19 pandemic was a harsh reminder that success without meaningful connections feels empty. In the pursuit of achievement, it's easy to overlook the importance of relationships, joy, and being fully present. True fulfillment comes not just from milestones but from the love, support, and shared experiences that make life meaningful. Take the time to prioritize human connections, cherish your loved ones, and redefine your success beyond mere accomplishments.

CHAPTER 9

Laying My Medical Affairs Foundations: A Journey of Purpose, Passion, and Perseverance

After completing my MBA, I found myself standing at a crossroads, not merely seeking a job, but also a deeper sense of purpose. My aspiration was to find a role that bridged the analytical rigor of my scientific background with my profound desire to make a meaningful impact on people's lives. With this vision in mind, I ventured into marketing, believing it could provide a unique avenue to influence healthcare in a positive and tangible way. During my internship, I was honored with the Outstanding Achiever Award for Marketing Excellence at a respected university hospital in New Jersey—a recognition that filled me with pride. Yet, despite this accomplishment, something within me remained unsettled.

While the recognition affirmed my competence, it did not bring the fulfillment I had hoped for. The work was important, and I excelled at it, but it lacked the depth of purpose I longed for. In marketing, the focus was on numbers—sales figures, market share, and profitability. But for me, success wasn't defined by metrics alone. I yearned to make a difference in patient care, not simply to sell a product. What I missed most was the scientific engagement—the data-driven insights, the research, and the direct impact on patients' lives.

The true nature of this disconnect became apparent during one meeting in particular. We were developing a campaign for a new medical device that was still in the early stages of clinical testing. Rather than discussing how the device could improve patient outcomes, the conversation was centered on how to position it for maximum sales potential. We discussed how quickly it could generate revenue, how it could reduce costs for hospitals, and how it compared to competing devices on the market.

It was at that moment that a realization struck me with startling clarity. Here I was, in a room full of brilliant people, discussing healthcare in terms that felt distant from the very purpose of medicine. The decisions we were making weren't about improving lives; they were about selling a product. I understood the importance and need of marketing in healthcare, but I couldn't reconcile it with my values. I missed the conversations that revolved around improving patient outcomes, where the focus was on care, science, and tangible results.

That experience was a turning point. It made me realize that I wasn't simply seeking professional success, but a career that aligned with my core values: a career where the focus was always on positively impacting patients' lives. I longed for a role where purpose was clear and where every decision contributed to advancing health, not just profits. I knew then that I needed to seek out a path that would bring me closer to that mission.

It was in moments of deep reflection—measuring not only my journey, but also the legacy of my mentor—that clarity began to emerge. I realized that my ambitions were not rooted solely in achievement, but in transformation. I wanted to contribute to something larger than myself: to reimagine how science, strategy, and empathy could intersect to reshape patient care. I wanted to play a role in shifting paradigms—bringing innovation to the forefront of treatment, amplifying the voice of the patient, and building bridges between scientific discovery and real-world healing.

This awakening didn't come with grand fanfare, but with a steady and unwavering resolve. A commitment to progress—to innovation with purpose—took root within me. And with it, the courage to leap. To embrace the challenge not as an obstacle, but as an invitation. An invitation to leave a legacy defined not just by milestones, but by meaning. A legacy of impact, service, and transformative change within the ever-evolving landscape of healthcare.

Then, fate intervened in a most unexpected way. One afternoon, while searching for a podcast to keep me company during my commute, I stumbled upon an episode that would change everything. It wasn't a podcast I'd planned to listen to, nor was it recommended by anyone. I had simply typed in "healthcare careers" on a whim, and the episode titled "The Role of Medical Affairs in Modern Healthcare" caught my eye.

The first few minutes were like an unfamiliar, yet welcoming, conversation—one that spoke directly to the blend of science, strategy, and business that I had been searching for. As I listened, I was introduced to the world of medical affairs, a field I had never previously considered. It was a revelation, a third pillar that seemed to connect everything I was passionate about. Unlike marketing—which felt disconnected from both patient care and pure science, and lacked the strategic impact I sought—medical affairs was the sweet spot. It bridged clinical knowledge with practical, real-world applications, all while ensuring that patient well-being remained at the forefront.

What truly captivated me during that episode wasn't just the technical aspects of the field, but the genuine passion of the speaker. They spoke about medical affairs as a role that not only influences the direction of healthcare but also actively shapes patient care and outcomes. The idea of working in a space where science, strategy, and patient advocacy intersect felt like an epiphany. It was as if I had found the missing piece I had been searching for.

One particular moment in the podcast stuck with me, like a feeling I couldn't shake. The speaker described how medical affairs professionals act as the bridge between clinical research and real-world healthcare, ensuring that the best scientific evidence is translated into meaningful patient solutions. In that instant, I realized that I was chasing a career that would enable me to use my scientific background in a way that directly impacted patients' lives, without abandoning the business acumen I had cultivated through my MBA. This was the perfect blend of both worlds.

The more I thought about it, the more this field resonated with my aspirations. Medical affairs wasn't about selling a product; it was about ensuring that every decision made in healthcare was informed by solid science and focused on improving outcomes. It wasn't just a job; it felt like a calling, one where I could contribute to the broader mission of bettering patient care on a meaningful scale.

That podcast didn't just spark curiosity; it ignited a fire within me. It was a turning point, a moment of clarity that reshaped my career trajectory. I immediately delved deeper into the field, reading articles, connecting with professionals in medical affairs, and gaining an understanding of the specific skills required for a role in this field. I realized this was the path that aligned with my values, background, and passion for patient-centered care.

I remember thinking, "This is it." I had found a career that seamlessly blended my scientific training with my desire to make a real difference in healthcare. It was a field that offered intellectual rigor and the opportunity to create a tangible impact, and it felt like the right place to bring my diverse experiences together. No longer did I feel adrift; I knew exactly where I was headed.

With unwavering conviction, I took a calculated risk and pursued a medical affairs role in one of the best consulting organizations in New York. After multiple rounds of interviews, rigorous presentations, and thought-provoking discussions, my dream materialized. The transition from the clinical realm to the business side of medicine was unconventional, but I always trusted my instincts. Determined to be part of this transformative field, I eventually joined the leadership team and immersed myself in work that felt aligned with my goals.

The leader of this organization hosted the very podcast that inspired me to take a leap into this field. To be inspired by a podcast and then ultimately join the very leader who sparked that inspiration is the kind of story many dream of. But I didn't just dream it; I strategically and successfully executed it. When I met the leader, I shared my journey with her, and at that moment, we formed an instant connection. She became my mentor, advocate, and cheerleader within the organization. I have always believed in the power of manifestation, but manifestation alone is not enough. You must pair it with an open mind, self-reliance, and unwavering determination. In other words, we can achieve anything if we are truly committed to it.

Once again, I followed my heart, and it led me to the right place. This consulting firm became my ultimate learning ground, a place where I committed to mastering every facet of medical affairs from the ground up. Working in this field opened a world of opportunities. I was regularly juggling multiple, very diverse projects. I gained hands-on experience working with different teams, engaging with experts, organizing key events, training professionals, simplifying scientific messages, collecting insights, studying the market, and coordinating all moving parts. I collaborated across R&D, commercial, and MedTech sectors, gaining a panoramic view of industry needs from global pharmaceutical giants to nimble startups.

The leadership team began to rely on my expertise, trusting me to execute complex initiatives with precision, delivering on time, within budget, and always at the highest level of quality. With each successful project, my capabilities became evident. However, what truly set my experience apart was the vastness of the field. It was an ocean that had never been confined to silos. Every challenge was reminiscent of my early days in oncology research—new terrains, steep learning curves, and an unrelenting demand for excellence.

The fast-paced world of consulting requires agility, high-quality deliverables, and the ability to pivot swiftly. I knew that if I was to make a meaningful impact and establish myself in a field as dynamic as medical affairs, my goal had to be clear: to develop a breadth of expertise that would position me as a true subject matter expert (SME).

In those early days, I quickly realized that to thrive in consulting, I would need to adapt rapidly and continuously expand my knowledge base. I was entrusted with oncology projects from the beginning because of my extensive training and deep-rooted passion for the field. The complexity of cancer care, the ever-evolving nature of treatments, and the urgent need for innovation kept me intellectually engaged. Over time, my focus sharpened, and I became an SME within "Oncology and Medical Affairs"—a field where precision, science, and patient outcomes intersect in profound ways.

One project, in particular, stands out. I was entrusted with leading a medical affairs initiative to organize and manage an advisory board for a new oncology therapy nearing regulatory approval. The goal was to gather input from key thought leaders and oncology specialists to shape the clinical development strategy and refine the drug's positioning within the healthcare system.

The challenge wasn't just understanding the clinical data; it was about translating that data into actionable insights that could guide not only the development process but also market access and patient outcomes.

I coordinated and facilitated discussions with experts to ensure that every aspect of the therapy— from clinical efficacy to patient access— was aligned with real-world needs.

Navigating through a maze of clinical evidence, emerging treatment paradigms, and regulatory considerations, I worked closely with the advisory board to evaluate the data from multiple perspectives. Our goal was to craft a strategy that was both scientifically robust and practical, ensuring that the therapy's eventual launch would meet the expectations of healthcare providers, payers, and, most importantly, the patients themselves.

After extensive hours of research, analysis, and collaboration, I synthesized the board's insights into strategic recommendations. These insights shaped the therapy's final positioning, influencing everything from clinical trial designs to post-market access strategies. Ultimately, the therapy was successfully adopted in several key markets, and our team's approach was credited with making a significant impact on the product's launch.

That experience solidified my expertise in oncology and medical affairs, empowering me to speak with authority on the complexities of the disease, its evolving treatments, and how healthcare policies intersect with patient access. It was through this advisory board work that I truly understood the importance of aligning scientific innovation with practical, patient-centered strategies.

But amid these professional triumphs, there was another reality I couldn't ignore—the delicate balancing act of being an ambitious working mother. Like so many working parents, there were days when the demands of project deadlines took precedence over bedtime stories, when client calls and urgent deliverables overshadowed precious moments with my growing child. I vividly remember one evening when I was working late to finalize a presentation for a critical client meeting. My daughter, then just a few years old, had been eagerly waiting for me to read her favorite bedtime story. I could hear her soft voice from the other room, saying, "Mama, come on!"

The tug-of-war between career and motherhood was ever-present. But through it all, I learned to be agile—not just in my professional life, but in my personal life as well. I became more strategic with my time, leveraging moments of flexibility when I could work from home or rearranging my schedule to attend important family events. I learned to be fully present when I was with my child, making those moments count, and to remain equally focused when I was in the office, giving my best to the work I was doing. It wasn't easy, but the ability to pivot quickly between my professional commitments and my family responsibilities became a skill in itself.

Ultimately, my time as a consultant, particularly in oncology, solidified my expertise and deepened my understanding of the intricacies of medical affairs. But perhaps more importantly, it taught me how to navigate the complexities of balancing career ambitions with family life, all while remaining agile, focused, and committed to both.

My husband, my unwavering support system, stepped in as he always does, helping to shoulder the responsibilities of parenthood. Still, I often question why ambitious mothers must navigate these impossible choices. Why does society not afford us an equal playing field, where the demands of work and family are shared equitably? The journey of a woman, mother, leader, and professional is often far steeper, far more exhausting. But I persisted, much like a duck, paddling furiously beneath the surface while maintaining a calm appearance above the water.

Each struggle reinforced my belief that growth often comes from discomfort, that success is not merely about milestones but about the impact we create. I embraced every aspect of medical affairs, absorbing knowledge like a sponge, eager to refine my craft. Every opportunity was a gift; every challenge a lesson. I transformed these learnings into powerful tools, and each one sharpened my ability to navigate the ever-evolving landscape of medical affairs. And on this journey, I didn't just grow; I evolved into a leader ready to shape the future of the field.

I left my career as an oncology scientist with a singular purpose: to serve a larger patient population and drive meaningful change in patient outcomes. Through every project I undertook, whether large or small, I felt empowered to fulfill that mission. Each opportunity was not merely a task; it was a service, a commitment to the patients affected by cancer. Completing a project successfully with full client satisfaction meant I was one step closer to making a tangible difference for those who desperately needed better treatments, improved regimens, and elevated standards of care. I was a person devoted to a mission, just as my name signifies. That profound sense of purpose became my guiding force.

To the ambitious women forging their paths in demanding fields, I offer this: cultivate a steadfast sense of self. Trust in your instincts; they are your compass. Recognize your worth, not through the lens of others, but through the quiet, unshakable knowledge of your own value. Honor that worth with intention, and love yourself enough to truly listen to the voice of reason, yes, but also to the quiet whispers of your heart.

In a world that often demands certainty, know that uncertainty is not your enemy; it is your proving ground. I've learned to welcome it with open eyes and a steady hand. I take calculated risks, not out of recklessness, but out of purpose. Each move thoughtfully mapped, each goal pursued with clarity and resilience. I design my game plans with care, prepare with discipline, and execute with determination. It is this alchemy—vision fused with strategy, and strategy fueled by persistence—that has carried me forward time and time again.

Success, in its traditional form, often follows. But when it doesn't, I've come to understand that the outcome is not failure; it is redirection. A gentle course correction from the universe, nudging me toward a better-aligned purpose and a greater truth.

One specific experience comes to mind while working on a project in medical affairs, particularly around the launch of a new oncology drug. We gathered a wealth of clinical data, developed a clear strategy, and engaged with leading oncologists to help refine our approach. Our goal was to help healthcare professionals understand how this new treatment could improve patient outcomes and offer them an alternative in cancer care.

However, when the drug was launched, we didn't see the level of adoption we had expected. Despite the strong evidence and our best efforts, some doctors were hesitant to use the treatment, and hospitals were slow to integrate it into their protocols. At first, I couldn't understand why the clinical data wasn't convincing enough. It felt like a setback.

Instead of viewing it as a failure, I saw it as an opportunity to re-evaluate. I reached out to healthcare providers, conducted primary research—spoke directly with oncologists, and asked for their feedback on what they were seeing and hearing. It became clear that while the drug had strong clinical benefits, we hadn't fully addressed some concerns. Doctors were unsure about the long-term impact of the treatment, and some weren't convinced about how it fit into the broader treatment plans they were already using.

So, we made adjustments. We refined our messaging to focus on the long-term benefits and real-world effectiveness of the drug. We engaged in more detailed conversations with medical experts and provided additional data that directly addressed their concerns. It took time, but gradually, doctors began to trust the treatment more and started using it in their practices.

In the end, the therapy was successfully adopted, but the journey to that success wasn't immediate. The real lesson I took away was that even in medical affairs, success doesn't always happen in a straight line. Sometimes, what appears to be a setback is just a moment that requires a deeper understanding and a chance to adjust course. By listening and adapting, we not only improved our strategy but also made sure we were truly addressing the needs of the patients and doctors we aimed to help.

The key, always, is momentum. Keep moving forward. When doors close, knock on others, or build new ones. Seek fresh opportunities with courage, grace, and relentless resolve. Let no setback define you. Let no obstacle diminish your light. And above all, never, ever give up. Your voice, your vision, and your presence matter more than you know.

The path to balancing family and career is rarely conventional. There will be moments of guilt, waves of doubt, and even flashes of frustration, but resilience is key. Stay focused, stay motivated, and push through the barriers that stand in your way. I do not advocate for rigidity or ruthlessness. Instead, I encourage seeking support, building a strong network, and leveraging resources because success should not be a solitary pursuit. Women deserve to achieve their ambitions with the same freedom and support as men.

We are not meant to carry the weight alone. We are meant to rise together, forging a path where fulfillment in both career and family is not just possible but expected.

After years of dedication in medical affairs—delivering high-impact outcomes, earning the trust of leadership, and mastering the nuanced complexities of the field—I arrived at an inflection point. I had proven myself in execution, in strategy, in shaping initiatives that moved the needle. But beneath the surface of professional accomplishment, a deeper calling stirred. I realized that my journey was no longer just about personal growth or even professional excellence. It was about purpose. About legacy. About impact.

I felt compelled to go beyond the bounds of tactical delivery and step into a role that allowed me to influence the very direction of medical affairs. I envisioned a space where I could help redefine its future, where the discipline could not only evolve but truly empower. That vision led me to embrace leadership roles where I could mentor others, nurture talent, and create environments that allowed both seasoned experts and newcomers to the field to thrive. I wanted to ensure that medical affairs professionals were equipped—not only with knowledge and resources—but with the confidence to lead, innovate, and elevate our collective mission in healthcare.

As I reflect on my journey, I can't overlook the challenges of being a woman and a mother in today's workplace. The balance between ambition and caregiving is a constant struggle, and it's not due to a lack of ability. It's because systems fail to support women in both roles.

Women are expected to excel in their careers while maintaining a perfect home life, but this invisible labor often goes unacknowledged. Workplaces treat caregiving as optional, rather than a lifelong responsibility. This is especially difficult in industries with long hours, regular travel, and high demands, where the system is designed for those without caregiving duties.

We need a shift in mindset. Workplaces must recognize caregiving as essential and not secondary. Women shouldn't have to choose between their careers and their responsibilities at home. It's time for change;

workplaces need to support women in balancing both, without compromising their success in either.

We need to reimagine professional ecosystems that not only acknowledge but support working mothers through flexible policies, inclusive leadership, and cultures that value empathy as much as performance. The future of medical affairs, and indeed any industry, must be built with equity at its foundation. Because when women—especially mothers—are empowered to succeed, they don't just change their own lives; they transform the world around them.

And that is the most enduring impact we can strive for.

True progress requires structural shifts, more flexible work arrangements, equitable parental leave policies, and a cultural transformation that normalizes caregiving as a shared responsibility, not just a woman's burden. Leaders and organizations must actively foster environments where women are not forced to choose between career advancement and family. Sponsorship, mentorship, and leadership development programs tailored for women can help break barriers, ensuring that talented professionals aren't sidelined simply because they are also mothers. For me, this isn't just an abstract goal. It's a responsibility.

By advocating for these changes, leading by example, and creating spaces where women feel seen, heard, and supported, I aim to contribute to a future where no woman has to sacrifice her aspirations due to systemic shortcomings. Women belong at the table, in the boardroom, and in leadership, and we must build the pathways that allow them to rise without compromise.

This journey is more than just the narrative of my own life; it is a reflection of a larger, shared truth. It is a testament to the strength, courage, and unwavering spirit of women who dare to carve out space for themselves in a world that often asks them to choose between ambition and caregiving, between self-fulfillment and self-sacrifice.

It is the story of every woman who rises each day determined to honor her dreams, even as she nurtures her family. It is a tribute to those who walk the delicate line between personal aspiration and collective responsibility, who balance boardroom decisions with bedtime stories, strategic plans with school runs, and professional growth with emotional presence.

There is immense power in resilience, in the quiet determination to keep going; to keep growing, no matter how winding the road. And there is profound beauty in reinvention, in the grace it takes to begin again, to shift course, to redefine success on one's own terms.

When we dare to listen to the quiet wisdom of our hearts and begin to trust in our own vast and often underestimated potential, something extraordinary happens: The boundaries we once accepted begin to dissolve. The world opens up. New paths emerge. And the possibilities become endless.

To every woman charting her course, know this: Your dreams are valid, your strength is immeasurable, and your story—whatever shape it takes—has the power to inspire. The sky is not the limit; it is only the beginning.

My message to all ambitious mothers who are working and striving for success in life: Please know that success is not just about career milestones, but about the impact we create and the lives we touch. Transitioning from research to medical affairs was a leap of faith, proving that growth comes from embracing discomfort and challenges. As ambitious women, we should not have to choose between our careers and our families. True progress comes when society supports both. Let's redefine success, uplift working mothers, and pursue our purposes with passion and perseverance.

CHAPTER 10

Breaking Barriers: A Woman's Journey to Serial Entrepreneurship and Growth in Medical Affairs

My journey into medical affairs began as an intellectual curiosity, a spark of interest that gradually blossomed into a deep, unwavering passion. As I immersed myself in the intricacies of this field, each project and each challenge became an opportunity for growth and discovery. The more I explored, the more I recognized the immense potential that medical affairs holds—not only in driving innovation but in bridging the gap between science and patient care.

With every initiative I led, I gained not only technical expertise but also a broader perspective on the complexities of the pharmaceutical landscape. I found myself becoming more attuned to the nuanced needs of both the industry and the healthcare system, seeing the challenges and opportunities that lie at the intersection of research, medicine, and patient outcomes.

My experiences working across a spectrum of organizations—ranging from industry giants to nimble startups—have afforded me a comprehensive understanding of the unmet needs within medical affairs. I've come to appreciate the delicate balance required in addressing these needs: ensuring that cutting-edge science translates into practical, accessible solutions for healthcare providers, while maintaining a relentless focus on improving patient outcomes. This work has enriched my expertise and deepened my commitment to contributing meaningfully to this vital field. Working with organizations from large industry leaders to agile startups has given me deep insight into the unmet needs within medical affairs.

This panoramic experience laid the foundation for a vision, one that extended beyond contributing to projects and into pioneering strategic solutions for the industry. With my deep expertise in research and development, oncology, marketing, and medical affairs, supported by a strong business acumen, I felt compelled to create something of my own.

I envisioned a firm that would not only provide strategic guidance and actionable insights but also help organizations transform challenges into opportunities. This vision propelled me to establish my unique boutique medical affairs consulting firm, where I could leverage my expertise to make a meaningful impact.

Within a year of launching my consulting firm, we partnered with a mid-sized biotech company based in the U.S. that was preparing to launch a novel targeted therapy for metastatic colorectal cancer. The science was strong, but they were struggling to position the therapy effectively in a crowded oncology space and engage the right stakeholders. The company hadn't fully integrated medical affairs into its launch planning.

Our team stepped in to build a comprehensive medical affairs roadmap from the ground up. We began by conducting KOL (Key Opinion

Leader) mapping and engagement planning, identifying the top 20 thought leaders in colorectal cancer across North America and Europe. Through a series of insight-generating advisory boards, we uncovered key knowledge gaps and regional variations in treatment adoption that were not captured in the clinical trial data.

From there, we designed MSL (Medical Science Liaison) training programs, tailored scientific and communication strategies. We supported the development of a compelling scientific narrative that positioned the company's therapy not just as a treatment, but as part of a broader precision medicine movement in GI oncology.

Just six months post-launch, the company had already surpassed its goal for the number of people who would start using the product within its first year.

More importantly, the therapy became a meaningful option for patients who had few alternatives—something the clinicians repeatedly expressed gratitude for during our follow-up insight rounds. That's where medical affairs shine, and this was the outcome of the collaboration with my company.

This project, among many others—both big and small—reminded me why I do what I do. Medical Affairs isn't just about data; it's about connecting science to impact. We sit at the intersection of clinical evidence, strategic communication, and real-world needs, bringing the voice of the patient and physician into every conversation that shapes a therapy's journey.

Never in my wildest dreams did I imagine that a girl who had once dared to dream big would one day be given the wings to soar. But I had an unwavering support system. My mother's belief in me, my husband's encouragement, my mentor's guidance, and my business partners' unwavering faith created an ecosystem that enabled me to pursue my dreams.

My success is not mine alone. It is a testament to the power of community, opportunity, and resilience. As I embraced my role as a CEO, an unexpected opportunity arose, one that further expanded my entrepreneurial journey. A distinguished medical oncologist from Boston approached me with the prospect of a strategic partnership.

Together, we co-founded a venture with a singular mission: to empower small and mid-sized healthcare technology companies, particularly those at the forefront of oncology. Our goal is to serve as a catalyst, accelerating transformative innovations from the initial stages of clinical development through to their successful integration into medical affairs. By bridging the gap between cutting-edge science and practical, market-ready solutions, we sought to drive meaningful progress in the oncology landscape, ensuring that groundbreaking therapies could reach the patients who needed them most, while also addressing the evolving needs of the healthcare ecosystem.

The realization of this partnership was beyond anything I could have ever imagined—a moment when one of my dreams became a reality. It was about more than just advancing oncology technologies; it was about transforming cutting-edge research into real-world solutions that could truly impact patients. By empowering small and mid-sized companies, we bridged the gap between innovation and practical application.

This venture also affirmed everything I had worked toward: combining my scientific background with my passion for medical affairs to drive meaningful change in healthcare. It was proof that with dedication and the right partnerships, dreams can evolve into powerful, transformative realities.

I remember telling my husband, "Pinch me. I don't want to wake up from this dream." His response was a reminder of the responsibility that comes with achievement: "With great success comes even greater responsibilities." Those words resonated deeply, grounding me in humility and gratitude.

Every single day, I wake up with an immense appreciation for the journey, recognizing that resilience, strategic perseverance, and self-belief are the keystones of success. Beyond my ventures, I found another avenue to expand my impact by associating myself with one of the most renowned medical affairs societies. This experience profoundly shaped my perspective on leadership. It showed me that while ambitious volunteers seek the guidance of great leaders, strong leaders also seek dedicated individuals who share their vision. Co-leading summits, moderating discussions, and networking with industry leaders across the country expanded my horizons in ways I had never imagined.

The desire to share knowledge and foster conversations in medical affairs led to yet another passion project. I created and host *The Medical Affairs Dialogues* podcast. This platform brings together industry leaders to discuss evolving trends, healthcare innovations, and the intersection of medical affairs with marketing, clinical, and project management. Through this initiative, I aim to unify and inspire both new and seasoned professionals, fostering a shared space for learning and collaboration.

Then came another moment of recognition and disbelief. In 2023, I was honored to be listed as an individual of distinction in the Marquis Who's Who in America, recognizing my significant contributions to the healthcare industry over the last decade. Marquis Who's Who is a prestigious biographical directory that recognizes exceptional professionals across diverse industries. Inclusion is a mark of distinction earned through a rigorous merit-based selection process that evaluates leadership, impact, career longevity, and contributions to society.

This recognition came as a complete surprise. Receiving this honor was a profound validation of my efforts, one that I accepted with deep gratitude and humility. Being selected for this honor strengthens my resolve to continue serving patients with the same passion, integrity, and purpose that have guided me from the very beginning. My dedication to patients was never driven by the pursuit of awards but by a genuine and unwavering commitment to making a difference. Still, the honor was truly humbling.

This journey is far from its final chapter. In truth, it is only the beginning—an unfolding, unfinished story woven with threads of resilience, ambition, and a relentless pursuit of purpose. Each step I've taken has been both a reflection of where I've come from and a compass guiding me toward where I'm meant to go. The road ahead remains unwritten, rich with promise and possibility.

As I look to the future, I do so with my head held high, grounded in hard-earned wisdom, yet uplifted by hope. My heart overflows with gratitude for the challenges that have shaped me, the mentors who have guided me, the loved ones who have stood by me, and the moments of quiet clarity that remind me of who I am.

Above all, I carry with me an unwavering belief in the boundless potential that lies ahead. When a woman dares to dream—unapologetically—and when the world around her believes in her as much as she believes in herself, there are no limits to what she can achieve. She doesn't simply chase success; she redefines it. She doesn't just rise; she lifts others with her. She doesn't merely build a future; she shapes it with vision, compassion, and indomitable strength.

As my now nine-year-old daughter, Aadrika, grows, I see the spark of possibility in her eyes—a reminder of why I do what I do. This past school year, in third grade, Aadrika excelled in math, science, music, and art. She got first place in both math and language in the I-Ready Challenge (a computer-based app), joined the school choir, and had a painting featured in the annual Art Show. Her leadership shone through in class presentations and at the International Food & Culture Fest. Outside school, she advanced in violin, performing at multiple showcases and was featured on the program cover. Her involvement in Girl Scouts, along with her passion for painting and pottery, highlights her creativity, independence, and leadership.

At this age, most students don't think to excel in such a wide array of activities, and quietly, it fills me with immense pride. Yet, I often find myself reflecting on how different her childhood is from mine in many meaningful ways. As a child, I was an all-rounder—curious, capable, and determined. But despite my achievements, I was rarely celebrated simply for being a girl. Gender was something I had to rise above, not something that added to my worth.

Now, I watch my daughter grow into her own brilliance, also an all-rounder, and I see something profoundly heartening: She is celebrated not just for what she does, but for who she is. Her identity as a girl is embraced and honored—every single day—within our home and in her immediate environment.

This shift didn't happen on its own. It began with my mother, who had the courage to challenge norms and make bold choices for me. Her quiet rebellion laid the foundation. And now, I carry that legacy forward, taking those strides even further, ensuring that the next generation doesn't just inherit a better world, but feels empowered to shape it with pride and freedom.

My husband and I are doing everything we can to offer her the opportunities to become the best version of herself and celebrate her presence in our lives, but I sometimes wonder: Will she truly appreciate these privileges? Will she take her opportunities seriously and make something meaningful of them?

I often ask her, just to understand her mindset, "Why are you doing all these things?" Her answer always warms my heart: "I've seen you help people, Mom. You always lift others up. I want to do the same. I want to be a doctor and help patients." It's clear that her actions aren't driven by a desire for accolades; they're fueled by a deep desire to create something greater than herself—a community of support and empowerment. She isn't just trying to excel in school or activities for the sake of it; she wants to make a lasting, positive impact.

Watching her lead with confidence and compassion in her school projects has been nothing short of magical. I see in her the same traits I've worked so hard to nurture in myself: the drive to break barriers, the desire to uplift others, and the belief that she, too, can shape the world around her.

In many ways, she's teaching me just as much as I am teaching her. She's learning that success isn't a solitary pursuit; it's about building something meaningful that helps others grow along the way. I can only hope that one day, when she reflects on her own path, she'll see that she was raised by a woman who didn't just dream big but showed her that dreams are meant to be lived with passion, purpose, and a heart full of compassion.

My entrepreneurial journey has been a profound learning experience, reshaping my definition of success along the way.

Initially, success for me was synonymous with accolades, achievements, and milestones. However, as I navigated the complexities of building something from the ground up, I realized that true success lies in the ability to create meaningful change, whether through empowering others, driving innovation, or improving lives. It's no longer about the destination but the impact made along the way, the trusted relationships built, and the resilience cultivated in the face of challenges.

To other women looking to break barriers in male-dominated industries, my advice is simple yet powerful: be unapologetically confident in your abilities, cultivate a strong support network, and never underestimate the power of perseverance. Don't shy away from being the first to take a seat at the table. When you do, make sure your voice is heard. The road won't always be easy, but resilience, coupled with a strategic mindset, will pave the way for you to thrive. Seek mentorship, stay focused on your goals, and embrace the courage to challenge the status quo.

As I envision the next chapter of my journey, my purpose has become even more deeply rooted in a commitment to uplift and empower women within the industry. What began as a personal pursuit of growth has evolved into a mission—one that intertwines entrepreneurial ambition with meaningful advocacy. I am more determined than ever to scale my ventures with intention, while using my voice and my podcast platform as a vehicle to amplify the stories that deserve to be heard, especially those of young girls and women forging their paths in healthcare and leadership.

(And yes—stay tuned for my next book.)

Looking ahead, I aspire to build a legacy defined not only by vision and enterprise but by empowerment, leadership, and enduring impact. I hope to be remembered not just as an entrepreneur who dared to dream beyond boundaries, but as a leader who made it her life's work to lift others as she climbed. A woman who challenged the status quo, dismantled barriers, and opened doors that were once closed, so that the path might be easier, freer, and more expansive for those who follow.

My greatest hope is that future generations of girls and women will inherit a world where their dreams are not confined by limitations but liberated by possibility. A world where they are seen, heard, and celebrated—for their intelligence, their courage, their compassion, and their power to lead. And if my journey contributes in some small way to that transformation, then that, to me, is a legacy worth leaving.

My message to women who dare to dream big: When you dare to dream and the world believes in you, there are no limits. Breaking barriers in medical affairs and entrepreneurship was not just about personal ambition for me. It was about creating impact, fostering innovation, and empowering others. Success is built on passion, resilience, and the courage to step into the unknown. By supporting and uplifting one another, we can redefine industries, inspire future leaders, and leave a lasting legacy. This journey is far from over. It's a testament to the power of perseverance and the limitless potential of women in leadership.

CHAPTER 11

Retrospection: Echoes of the Past

I am deeply fulfilled knowing that I've accomplished more than I set out to achieve. However, with each new accomplishment, my definition of success evolved, and I feel that with every new step, there are always new peaks to conquer, new challenges to rise to.

I often still feel the need to impress others with my achievements, milestones, and accolades; I'm only human, after all. Despite everything I've accomplished, it's hard to resist the expectations of others. How do I navigate these pressures? Most importantly, am I setting the right example for my daughter? I do my best, every day, to play some small part in creating a world where young girls and women don't have to endure the struggles I faced. I am not perfect, but this is always what I strive toward.

Looking back at the way society treated my family because my mother could not bear a son, I now understand the deeply ingrained biases that shape people's actions and words. They didn't know better, and no one was challenging the status quo. It takes women like us—brave, relentless trailblazers—to push against the grain and create new opportunities.

By doing so, we empower countless young girls to dream big and dream fearlessly. If I could speak to my younger self, I would say: Trust your instincts, be brave, and take those bold steps. The road ahead will be very tough. Brace yourself for the challenges. However, remember that you are destined to break societal norms and lead by example. You will inspire others, paving the way for generations of girls and women to follow. Stay true to your beliefs and don't let anyone or anything sway you. You are meant to keep the ball rolling, create history, and, above all, take the world by storm. More power to you!

The following section offers a series of reflective questions—ones I've thoughtfully considered myself, and ones I invite you to explore as well. Taking time to reflect on your personal beliefs in these areas can illuminate your potential to become a catalyst for meaningful change, not just in your own life, but in the lives of other women around you.

Can a woman succeed without external support, or is that an illusion society sells us? How do we create self-sufficiency while still recognizing the power of community?

The path to success for a woman is often steep and laden with challenges. Unwavering focus, self-motivation, and resilience can propel her toward her mission, but no woman climbs that mountain alone. Behind every milestone stands a village of unwavering support. The truth is that she cannot "have it all" without the right people by her side, creating an ecosystem that nurtures her growth and sets her up for success in all stages of life. I cannot emphasize this enough.

To the parents of daughters—the girls you've nurtured, cherished, and proudly called the apple of your eye—your support must not end when she steps into adulthood or marriage. Stand by her, not just in the early chapters, but throughout her journey. Do not leave her dreams at the mercy of others who may not recognize her worth. You have invested your love, time, and hope in her; continue to advocate for her, fiercely and consistently, as she strives to build a life of purpose and fulfillment.

For men, their support systems—mothers, wives, and families—stand steadfast alongside them, ensuring that their dreams are realized. Inherently, as a society, we value and celebrate the life of a boy more than that of a girl. How many fearless mothers champion their daughters' ambitions with the same grit? How many husbands stand on the sidelines, cheering as their wives strive on the path to success?

As a society, we still grapple with deeply rooted hypocrisies. As a woman ascends the ladder of success, she might find the voices of her cheerleaders growing fainter. Insecurities, personal ambitions, and unforeseen distractions can cause even the most trusted supporters to drift away. This is why a woman must build a foundation that is reliant on her "village."

True success for a woman lies not only in having a strong support system but also in the ability to stand tall and flourish, even when she must walk alone. At this point, it reminds me of the words of Rabindranath Tagore, a very famous poet and Nobel Laureate from India, who said, "If nobody comes with you, do not lose hope. Walk away alone, and you will still succeed." This is the mantra for a girl who has the mark of a survivor, a trailblazer, a woman who defies the odds to create her destiny.

For women and girls who don't have parental or spousal support, what alternatives do they have? How can they cultivate their sources of strength? What systemic changes need to happen so that all women, regardless of background, have a fair chance of success?

This is a challenging topic, and it bothers me every day. It's something that many women all over the world grapple with. There is no definitive right or wrong way to build your "village," the support system that fortifies your journey. If you don't have parental or spousal support, consider reaching out to your community. Are there organizations or groups that can provide support and resources? Strength is fortified when we lean on each other. One thing is certain: to truly succeed, you need a foundation—pillars of support, whether familial or not. This kind of support is so naturally granted to boys and men. Why not to women?

Too often, women find themselves crushed under the weight of relentless pressures, professional demands, societal expectations, and the invisible yet all-consuming responsibilities that come with simply existing in a world that still resists their ascent. Without a steady, quickly responsive support system, even the most ambitious and resilient women—those who once carved out promising paths for themselves—may find their strength eroding. The burden becomes too heavy, the fractures too deep, and the once unshakable spirit begins to break.

This is a great challenge, the unspoken barrier, an emotional and structural imbalance that forces many women to yield, not because they lack talent or determination, but because they were never given the same help to endure when the winds of adversity came howling.

Until we address this fundamental inequality, true and sustained success for women will remain an uphill battle, one that demands not just personal resilience but a collective shift in how we nurture and sustain the dreams of those who dare to rise.

What advice would you give to those women trying to preserve their authentic selves while embracing new worlds?

I have undergone numerous transformations and cultural transitions, which have shaped me into a true global citizen. Time and again, I have demonstrated immense grit and adaptability, embracing new languages, customs, and countries with an open heart.

For me, home transcends geography; it resides in the land where I was born and nurtured, in the nation that shaped my professional path, and in the country that gave me a voice, recognition, and a profound sense of belonging. Each place is woven into the fabric of my identity. And all people—regardless of race, background, or color—are my people. As a healthcare professional, I believe every patient is deserving of equal dignity, thoughtful attention, and compassionate care.

At no point in my journey have I felt that I lost my identity. Rather, every cultural thread I've encountered has become an essential part of my tapestry—adding nuance, depth, and vibrancy to who I am. Each experience has not diminished me but refined me, broadening my perspective and expanding my capacity for empathy. These layers have not blurred my essence; they have illuminated it, enriching my understanding of the world and deepening my connection to the shared humanity we all carry.

The greatest gift you will ever possess is yourself. Embrace your essence with reverence, nurture your growth with intention, and allow yourself the grace to evolve. Be unapologetically authentic, for everyone else is already taken, and the world needs the singular brilliance that only you can offer.

Motherhood has deepened my understanding of identity, roots, and legacy. Through my daughter's eyes, I see anew the sacred responsibility of honoring where we come from while envisioning where we are going. I hope she grows up embracing the best of both worlds—the timeless wisdom and soulful richness of Indian culture, and the progressive, boundary-breaking spirit of the West. To become a true "global citizen" it does not demand to choose between cultures, but to let them converge into something uniquely personal—an identity forged from inclusion, not division.

This is the message I carry, not just for my daughter, but for every young girl navigating the tender space between her heritage and her aspirations. May they rise with pride in their lineage, rooted yet unbound, confident in their complexity, and fearless in their dreams. Let them know they do not need to conform to a singular mold to belong. Their power lies in the full spectrum of who they are—in every layer, every origin, every possibility.

Do you ever wonder if you have sacrificed too much? What are the hidden costs of ambition—mentally, emotionally, and physically?

There are moments when I pause and wonder: Has life demanded too much of me? It's a question that lingers in quiet contemplation, yet one I may never truly know. Every step I have taken—every decision I have made—has been a conscious choice. I did not stumble upon this path; I carved it, knowingly and purposefully.

And would I change any of it? No, not for a moment. I would relive each chapter, both the bitter and the sweet, the triumphs and the trials. These experiences—raw, unfiltered, and often unforgiving—have sculpted the woman I am today, both in my personal essence and in my professional strength.

The journey has tested me mentally, emotionally, and physically. At times, it has felt like walking through fire. But even fire refines. And perhaps the true measure of a life well lived is not found in ease, but in the resilience to rise, to evolve, and to find grace amid the weight of it all.

After all, what we perceive as hardship is often nothing more than perspective—and from where I stand now, every struggle was a lesson, every scar a story, every detour a re-direction toward something greater.

If you aim for the sky, you must understand that there is a price to pay. The price that we each pay is different, depending on our circumstances, our support networks, and the choices that we make. I chose to pay the prices that I have paid over the years. I have learned a lot along the way, and I'm grateful for the lessons and the growth.

Still, I fear that if I take a professional pause, I will risk becoming irrelevant, cut out of the value chain, and on a path of no return. This is the harsh reality many women face. We are constantly pushing, striving, and forcing change with the hope that the sacrifices we make will create a smoother road for the next generation of girls.

To every woman standing at the edge of burnout: pause, breathe. Gently turn inward and give yourself the care and compassion you so readily offer to others. Prioritize self-preservation not as an indulgence, but as a necessity. Practice self-love as a daily ritual, not a distant reward. And when the weight feels too heavy, do not hesitate to reach out. Asking for help is not a sign of weakness; it is a courageous act of strength and self-awareness. You are worthy of support, not because you are struggling, but because you are human.

Take time to step back and reflect—not just once, but often. Reassess your path, your happiness, and whether your life remains in harmony with your values and goals. Realignment is not a setback; it is a vital part of the growth process. And as you do this, remember the power of boundaries. Setting and honoring them is essential, not only for your physical health, but for your mental clarity and emotional well-being. Boundaries are not walls; they are acts of love that protect your energy and preserve your peace.

In a world that often demands more than it gives, let this be your reminder: You do not need to burn out to prove your worth. You are already "enough"—just as you are.

Some sacrifices are worth making to reach your goals. But that doesn't mean you have to do things "the way they've always been done." Ambition also means learning, shifting, and growing. Those of us in the sandwich generation can pass on the valuable lessons we've learned from our parents about resilience, and we can also share our own lessons learned along the way, such as speaking up for ourselves, demanding a seat at the table, and even creating our own tables. Sharing this with our children and acting as mentors when possible will make this transformation happen for the women who come after us. Until then, we keep pushing forward, not just for ourselves but for the future we envision.

What is the truest, deepest form of success for you today?

In the past, my accomplishments, accolades, and awards have often defined me and served as a measure of my success. This has been by design and necessity, shaped by the lack of precedent and the pioneering nature of each milestone I've achieved, often with limited resources. This is how I have defined my journey.

Yet beyond the titles, milestones, and accolades, what truly drives me now is a deeper calling—a desire to leave a meaningful and enduring impact on the lives of patients and to inspire the next generation of girls to lead with confidence, purpose, and a heart. Over time, my perspective has shifted—from an "achievement-based mindset" rooted in metrics and milestones to one that prioritizes "fulfillment and impact" model. I now seek satisfaction, significance, and genuine contribution.

Though I have often measured success by what I could accomplish, I now find myself drawn to the quiet satisfaction that comes from purposeful work—the kind that resonates at a soul level. True success, I've come to realize, is not about perfection or the destination; it is about presence, growth, and intention. It is about redefining what it means to live a successful life: one that values purpose over performance, joy over just outcomes, and connection over comparison. It is a journey of cultivating well-being, practicing self-love, and building authentic, meaningful relationships along the way.

I am only at the beginning of creating the impact I envision. There is still so much ground to cover, so many lives to touch, and stories yet to be written. The next chapter of my legacy is devoted to building a "value-based foundation" for young girls and women aspiring to lead in medical affairs with meaningful partnerships. I want to create a space where they are seen, supported, and empowered—not only with skills and knowledge, but with the confidence to lead unapologetically and the freedom to honor both their professional ambitions and personal truths.

My mission is to nurture a generation of women leaders who no longer have to choose between career and care, between excellence and well-being, but who can instead thrive at the intersection of both.

Regarding women in leadership and entrepreneurship, is the path open for the next generation?

The world must become one where women are offered as many chances as men, where there is room for them to have a seat at the table, both at home and in the boardroom. This reality, both in the East and the West, needs to change. I'm not against men's privileges, but I'm advocating for a more equal playing field where all individuals can co-exist and prosper.

I want to see a society where women can not only dream of "having it all" but actually achieve their desires. This is the new mission I have embarked upon, one that is unfinished and one I will continue to pursue with all my heart.

While progress has been made, barriers still exist. The next generation will have it easier but will continue to face societal and systemic challenges. What still needs to change? A shift in culture and organizational structures is needed, creating inclusive, family-friendly environments and dismantling outdated gender roles. More accessible mentorship and networking opportunities are crucial.

How can more women enter leadership without unsustainable expectations?

The prevailing culture surrounding the "ideal worker" is long overdue for a thoughtful redefinition. For too long, professional success has been modeled on outdated paradigms that assume constant availability, rigid schedules, and a singular, linear career path—often shaped around the traditional male experience. This model not only marginalizes working mothers but overlooks the richness and diversity of modern workforces.

It is time for organizations to adopt more flexible, humane, and forward-thinking approaches, ones that acknowledge the complexities of life beyond the office. A wealth of research supports the benefits of flexible work arrangements, including increased productivity, better retention, higher employee satisfaction, and improved mental well-being. Yet, what's often lacking is the will to reimagine the system.

We must move away from the antiquated notion that women are primarily homemakers while men are the default breadwinners. This binary not only limits women's potential but also undermines the evolving roles of men in family life. Supporting working mothers should not be a token gesture; it must be a structural commitment.

Policies such as extended paid maternity and paternity leave, accessible and affordable childcare, and pathways to leadership that actively promote women into decision-making roles are not luxuries; they are necessities.

By championing these changes, companies do more than revise their policies; they redefine their culture. They send a resounding message: that women's contributions are not only acknowledged but genuinely valued, not merely in words, but in action. That women are not expected to stretch themselves to the brink, constantly proving their worth through unsustainable effort, but are instead provided with the structures and support they need to truly flourish.

This is not solely a matter of gender equity; it is a call to build a workplace that reflects the realities of modern life, one that is compassionate, resilient, and inclusive by design. When organizations embrace flexibility, elevate diverse voices, and invest in policies that support both personal and professional well-being, they pave the way for a new era of leadership—one where success is measured not by sacrifice, but by balance; not by endurance, but by empowerment.

In such a future, all individuals, regardless of gender, can harmonize the roles they hold in life with dignity, authenticity, and purpose. This is the kind of transformation that doesn't just benefit women; it elevates everyone.

One powerful step you can take today is to assert your voice and own your value. Speak with intention. Seek out leadership opportunities, even when the path is not clearly marked. Advocate for yourself unapologetically, and never diminish your accomplishments to make others feel more comfortable. Let your confidence reflect the truth of your journey—hard-earned, deeply felt, and fully deserved.

Stay rooted in your authenticity, guided by your purpose, and anchored in a strong sense of self. True leadership is not about conforming to established molds; it's about boldly shaping new ones. It's about forging your own path, grounded in resilience and clarity, and recognizing that your unique perspective is not only valid but vital. Embrace the impact only you can make, and step forward not just with ambition, but with conviction and grace.

Now that you've achieved what once felt impossible, what's next?

The next chapter of my life is one of purpose and promise, devoted to realizing a dream I have long cherished: empowering women in leadership, particularly within the field of medical affairs. It is a mission born from both personal conviction and lived experience, one that calls me to create a safe, inclusive, and empowering environment where young girls can thrive, pursue their passions, and see no limits to what they can become.

I am especially driven to shape this future for the next generation of girls, not only as a professional, but as a mother. My vision for change is anchored in something far greater than myself. As global icon Priyanka Chopra Jonas once said in an interview, "I want to see more brown faces, women with brown faces up there on stage." That sentiment struck a profound chord in me. I, too, long to see more brown women faces, not only on stages but at boardroom tables, in C-suites, at global forums—spaces where decisions are made and voices matter.

This journey has become more than personal; it has become a call to collective action. It's about redefining representation, dismantling barriers, and uplifting the girls of tomorrow who deserve to see themselves reflected in positions of influence and power. It's about nurturing leadership that doesn't ask women to choose between their identity and their aspirations but celebrates both.

Through my ventures—my consulting companies and my podcast platform—I am committed to amplifying these voices, creating spaces where stories are shared, perspectives are honored, and opportunities are unlocked. I want to inspire women to claim their space, advocate for one another, and lead with authenticity, empathy, and strength.

And this is only the beginning. I am steadfast in my resolve to turn this vision into reality, not just for myself, but for every woman who dares to dream, and for every young girl who is watching, waiting, and ready to rise.

How do self-motivation and support systems fit in with the desire to "have it all"?

To the world, my story might seem like a picture of success, an inspiring journey that appears seamless, even enviable.

My girlfriends who have watched me for many years now often tell me, "You have it all," but the reality is far more complicated. It is a path marked by solitude, relentless perseverance, and an unyielding commitment to self-motivation every single day. It may seem as though I thrive because of a vast support system, but the truth is more nuanced.

The support I have is not a privilege bestowed upon me; it is something I have carefully nurtured over time. Those who stand by me are people I deeply cherish, but they are not flawless. They have their struggles, as well as their highs and lows. As a woman grows and her influence shifts, so, too, can the dynamics of the relationships around her. Support is never guaranteed. It evolves, sometimes wanes, and can even disappear entirely.

This has taught me an invaluable lesson. I am grateful for the support I receive, but I never depend on it. I have seen loved ones step away, not out of malice but because life demanded their attention elsewhere. So, I have learned to remain open to change, to accept that support is fluid, but never to tether my sense of stability to any one person.

True resilience comes from cultivating self-reliance. However, even in self-reliance, one must acknowledge that no great journey is undertaken alone. Throughout life, we will always need allies, mentors, and companions. The key lies in recognizing who might stand beside us in moments of need while also being prepared to offer them the same in return.

Life is not a game of defectors. In the intricate dance of game theory, it is the cooperative player who ultimately triumphs, though cooperation demands its own price. It calls for time, patience, and the deliberate, often slow work of building trust. Above all, I aspire to cultivate this kind of trust with my daughter: to be her unwavering pillar of support, just as I hope she will be mine, not out of obligation, but rooted in mutual faith, unconditional love, and an unbreakable partnership.

Then, there is my husband—a rare man endowed with the empathy to perceive the silent struggles that women face daily. Yet how many men truly share this mindset? Far too few. Raised within societal frameworks that seldom nurture such qualities in boys, many men grow up without understanding that supporting women is a profound strength. Consequently, these quiet champions often stand isolated, lacking role models, enduring unspoken judgment from peers, and sometimes carrying the heavy burden of shame for defying convention.

We must elevate their voices, celebrate their efforts, and crown them as the emblematic allies of a movement dedicated to normalizing men's vital role in championing women's growth and leadership. By doing so, we can spark a transformation that not only empowers women but also liberates men from the confines of outdated expectations, paving the way for a more balanced and compassionate world—one worthy of our daughters' future.

How can mothers shape the next generation?

Children are bound to their mothers by an invisible thread—an umbilical cord of love and sacrifice that endures far beyond birth. I have felt the profound depth of this connection: A silent, unyielding force that weaves mother and child together in ways words can scarcely capture. For most mothers, the choice to prioritize their child's needs is seldom a true choice at all; it is an expectation, deeply embedded in the very fabric of society.

Some embrace this role willingly, finding fulfillment and a sense of identity in caregiving. Others wrestle with the quiet heartbreak of stepping away from careers they have nurtured with years of dedication, passion, and ambition. Across cultures and continents—whether East or West—the expectation remains stubbornly unchanged: A mother must put her child first, often at the expense of her own dreams. A career, once a source of purpose and identity, is dismissed as though it were disposable—like an "used tissue"—a fleeting phase to be outgrown. But does society demand the same sacrifice of fathers? Are men expected to relinquish their professional pursuits with the same ease and inevitability? Certainly not.

This disparity weighs heavily on me. I witness how my daughter's expectations of me are markedly greater than those she holds for her father. It is I who must guide, discipline, and mold her into the woman she is becoming. I am the one who must say "no," who teaches resilience, kindness, and integrity. In this dynamic, I have become the "bad cop," while my husband takes on the role of the "good cop," the one who plays, indulges, and escapes the burden of correction. I worry that this imbalance may one day estrange her from me. Will she resent me for being the enforcer of rules? Will she mistake discipline for a lack of warmth or love? Yet if I step back from this role, if I choose only to be the comforting presence, who will prepare her for the realities of the world?

In these moments, I find myself reflecting on my mother and the quiet sacrifices she made that I once failed to recognize. My father was the provider; his worth was measured by his financial contributions. My mother was the foundation—her strength unseen, her labor unpaid, her presence undervalued. As a child, I equated importance with earning power, overlooking the immeasurable impact of my mother's wisdom, steadfastness, and devotion. Only when I became a mother did I begin to truly grasp the magnitude of her power.

Unlike her generation, I am acutely aware of my worth. The world assigns a price to my time, but I insist on being valued not just in the professional realm, but within my own home. Still, I wonder: Does my daughter see me as inferior because I am more available to her? Does she assume, as I once did about my mother, that my presence signals a lesser standing in my career? Or will she come to understand the delicate equilibrium I strive to maintain—the sacrifices made not from obligation, but from love—and recognize that this balance is my way of prioritizing her?

We have made progress, yes, but the journey is far from complete.

Crucial questions remain unanswered: How do mothers like me maintain a sense of self-worth while balancing the immense responsibilities of career and family? How do we raise our daughters to claim their value boldly, to demand what they deserve, and to navigate the relentless pressures of excelling in multiple spheres without losing themselves in the process? More importantly, how do we reshape this path so it becomes less of a burden and more of a source of fulfillment, so that our daughters, alongside our sons, can walk through life with confidence, joy, and the freedom to forge their own definitions of success without sacrificing one part of themselves for another?

Can women truly "have it all" without the accompanying pain?

It is time to rewrite the narrative, not just for us, but for the generations yet to come. A narrative where ambition and nurture coexist, where professional achievement and personal fulfillment are not mutually exclusive, and where the next generation of girls can rise with strength, clarity, and the unwavering belief that they deserve nothing less than a life wholly their own.

If there are so many hardships that women have to go through, why try to "have it all"?

The notion of "having it all" is often dismissed as an unattainable ideal—a myth perpetuated by unrealistic expectations and cultural narratives that leave many women feeling pressured and overwhelmed. Yet, it is crucial to understand that "having it all" need not equate to perfection or flawless balance in every aspect of life. For women, the challenges are indeed real, and the weight of societal demands can feel crushing at times. But striving to "have it all" is not about chasing an impossible ideal; it is about defining success on your own terms—shaped by your values, dreams, and deepest priorities.

Why pursue this quest? Because every woman deserves the opportunity to chase her ambitions freely, to build a career that inspires her, to love fiercely, nurture her family, and create a life rich with purpose and fulfillment. The hardships we encounter along the way do not diminish us; rather, they forge resilience, deepen wisdom, and fuel growth. Each obstacle, each sacrifice, becomes a stepping stone that refines our strength and shapes the future we envision.

By embracing this mindset, we reclaim the narrative of "having it all" from the confines of societal expectation and recast it through the lens of our own strength, resolve, and intention. It is not a pursuit of perfection, but a commitment to perseverance. It is the courage to find joy in the journey—amidst the messiness and uncertainty—and the belief that we are fully capable of crafting lives imbued with meaning, success, and authentic fulfillment.

The path is seldom easy, and the balance is rarely seamless. But the effort to live a life truly your own—defined not by others but by yourself—is a worthy endeavor. It is in this courageous pursuit that we unlock the profound truth: "Having it all" does not mean having everything, but rather having enough of what matters most. And that is a power and grace all women deserve to claim.

Conclusion

To My Dear Readers:

This book is dedicated to you—the curious minds, the lifelong learners, the quiet seekers of wisdom who dare to ask questions, to dream deeply, and to pursue growth not merely as a goal but as a way of life. Your presence within these pages is not something I take lightly. It is a gift, a quiet act of trust, and for that, I am profoundly grateful.

Whether you find yourself drawn here by curiosity, seeking inspiration, or yearning for deeper understanding, know that your engagement gives this work its true purpose. Your willingness to explore these ideas, to reflect, and to be present in this shared space of thought and inquiry elevates every word on the page. Thank you for being here.

As we navigate the complexity and velocity of modern life, we often encounter the pervasive idea of "having it all"—a phrase that promises fulfillment but often masks the invisible sacrifices, relentless pressures, and quiet endurance required behind the scenes. The illusion of perfect balance can leave us feeling inadequate, chasing ideals not our own.

True fulfillment, I've come to believe, is not found in checking every box or achieving every milestone dictated by others. It lives in the freedom to define success for ourselves—honestly, unapologetically, and in alignment with our inner compass. It is shaped by the strength of our self-motivation and held up by the quiet power of the support systems we build and nurture.

In this redefinition of success, let us pause to honor those who walk beside us: the parents and partners who believe in us, the mentors who light our paths, the friends and communities who uplift us in seen and unseen ways. These are the pillars that sustain us. And as we draw strength from them, so too must we strive to become such pillars for others—to uplift, to support, and to ensure that those who follow in our footsteps inherit not just the pressure to achieve, but the wisdom to create lives of authenticity, meaning, and joy.

Let us continue to challenge the narratives that confine us, to expand the boundaries of what is possible, and to embrace the evolving, expansive nature of fulfillment. The future before us is not a fixed destination but a canvas—alive with possibility, rich with opportunity, and waiting for the mark only you can make.

Now is the time to claim that future. Step forward with courage, clarity, and the conviction that you are capable of building a life that reflects who you truly are. Let go of outdated expectations. Define success on your own terms. Let your story be one of self-discovery, resilience, and purpose.

May this journey inspire you to continue growing, not just upward, but inward. May you dream boldly, give generously, support one another fiercely, and never stop learning. The path ahead belongs to you, and the extraordinary is within reach. Let us walk it together.

Let's connect and share the journey. The possibilities are endless, and I would love to continue this conversation with you.

Incentive - 1: "A Seat at the Mic": Join me on the podcast

If you are inspired by what you have read and would like to share your own story, I'd be thrilled to feature you as a guest on my podcast, *Inspiring Women Stories*. Reach out to me at Inspiringwomenstories1@gmail.com, and let's explore how your journey can inspire others.

Incentive - 2: Free Companion Workbook: "Reflect, Rewrite, Rise"

A Guided Journal for Turning Insight into Action: This downloadable PDF workbook is your personal sanctuary for reflection, healing, and growth as you journey through the stories in the book. Use it as a companion after each chapter or all at once—there is no right or wrong way to engage. Let it hold your thoughts, honor your experiences, and guide your steps forward.

Together, we can create an experience that challenges perspectives and drives meaningful change. Feel free to contact me. I look forward to connecting and exploring what we can achieve together.

With gratitude and unwavering hope:

– Bratati Ganguly, PhD, MBA, BCMASc

THANK YOU FOR READING MY BOOK!

DOWNLOAD YOUR FREE GIFTS

Thank You for Your Support

As a heartfelt thank you for purchasing and reading my book, I'd love to offer you a few special bonus gifts—completely free, with no strings attached. It's my way of showing appreciation for your time, your curiosity, and your support.

Enjoy—and thank you again for being part of this journey.

Scan the QR Code:

I appreciate your interest in my book and value your feedback, as it helps me improve future versions. I would appreciate it if you could leave your invaluable review on Amazon.com with your feedback. Thank you!

www.ingramcontent.com/pod-product-compliance
Lightning Source LLC
Chambersburg PA
CBHW062107080426
42734CB00012B/2781